westland ltd
DELHI: 14 HISTORIC WALKS

Swapna Liddle studied history, getting her doctorate for a thesis on nineteenth-century Delhi. Beginning as a casual interest, the protection of Delhi's old buildings developed into a passion. For some years now, she has been organizing and leading walks around the historic precincts of the city for the India Habitat Centre and the Indian National Trust for Art and Cultural Heritage (INTACH). She is also closely involved with INTACH's heritage protection and public awareness programmes.

D1571276

DELHI
14 HISTORIC WALKS

Swapna Liddle

westland

westland ltd

Venkat Towers, 165, P.H. Road, Maduravoyal, Chennai 600 095

No. 38/10 (New No.5), Raghava Nagar, New Timber Yard Layout, Bangalore 560 026

Survey No. A - 9, II Floor, Moula Ali Industrial Area, Moula Ali, Hyderabad 500 040

23/181, Anand Nagar, Nehru Road, Santacruz East, Mumbai 400 055

4322/3 Ansari Road, Daryaganj, New Delhi 110 002

First published in India by westland ltd 2011

ISBN: 978-93-81626-24-5

Design & Layout by Manav Agarwal

Printed at Manipal Technologies Ltd., Manipal

For my mother, from whom I learnt a love for language, and my father who taught me that anything worth doing is worth doing with a passion.

ACKNOWLEDGEMENTS

Neither the walks nor this book would have been possible without the help of a large number of people. Many years ago it was Arshiya Sethi who first suggested that I could lead walks around historic sites in Delhi. Prof Narayani Gupta, apart from being a guide and mentor, introduced me to INTACH. Renu Oberoi and Shivani Darbari have helped me to be a part of the walks programme at the India Habitat Centre. A number of people at INTACH—Ajay Kumar, Priya Sinha and the other dedicated walk leaders have lent their support and taught me much. I must also thank the hundreds of people who have joined me for a walk—they are the reason to keep doing walks, and are frequently the source of new pieces of information.

Delhi: 14 Historic Walks in particular, would not have come about without the initial suggestion from Renuka Chatterjee, the hard work of Jaya Bhattacharji Rose and Manav Agarwal, and my sister, Madhulika Liddle, who took lovely photographs—thank you all.

COME WALK WITH ME

This book is the outcome of years of walking through historic areas in Delhi. I have walked alone, with friends, leading organized heritage walks, or on walks led by others. Through books and other people's walks, I have discovered many areas, that have not only led me to interesting places but also helped me understand the history behind the buildings.

It has been a long journey, and it is by no means over. I have a suprisingly long list of places that I am either still to visit or have not visited in a long time. I am constantly getting fresh perspectives on the well-worn trails by new discoveries in the library.

I hope this book will tempt others to find equal pleasure in the historic walks that I have found, without having to either join an organized walk, or having to do extensive research for reliable historical information. The fourteen walking routes in Delhi included in this book are tried and tested. Some are through areas that are very well known and are

ticketed historic attractions, including the three World Heritage Sites—Qutub Minar complex, Humayun's Tomb and Red Fort. Others, such as Khirki or Mehrauli village, are relatively unknown, except perhaps to those living in the immediate vicinity.

My excuse for including the very well-known tourist sites is that the information provided by the signs or tourist guides are either frustratingly inadequate, or more seriously, wildly inaccurate. Yet these are fascinating places with great historical significance. For the less well-known areas, often these are buildings that are in the neighbourhood, or beside the road but information at these sites is often inadequate, if it exists at all.

The selection criteria for each route in this book was first and foremost that there should be enough to see so that it is rewarding. There should be an interesting story behind the buildings and/or a background history of the area, tying them together. It should be a fairly pleasant walk—I have left out the particularly litter-strewn or overgrown paths. I have also tried to include only those buildings that are easily accessible to the public. Nothing can be more frustrating than to read about a wonderful place, only to discover that it cannot be visited. The status of the buildings does however keep changing. So readers, please forgive me, if a building accessible at the time of going to print has subsequently become inaccessible.

The walking routes charted out here will lead you clearly through an area, helping you find your way around and identify each building. Each walk will tell you about the historical background of the site that you are visiting, quite apart from the individual buildings within it. At each building it will tell you its history to the extent that it is known. It will also point out significant architectural and decorative

features, and the concepts and techniques that lay behind them. *Delhi: 14 Historic Walks* intends to go further than the average guide book; I have tried to incorporate insights that are rarely known beyond academic publications. Before this frightens off the lay reader, I hasten to add that I have done this in an easy-to-read style.

The walks are arranged in a roughly chronological order—oldest areas to newest. I say, 'roughly', because in most areas there are buildings dating from different times. On the whole, however, the idea is that if you proceed from one to the next in an orderly fashion you will get a systematic history of the development of the city and its architectural heritage. Of course this is not essential. Each walk stands alone, and if you have the time or inclination for even just one, go ahead and pick any.

At the beginning of each walk I have included some practical information such as timings and the rate of tickets. Other helpful tips to ease your way through particular areas include maps, an essential tool for navigating the areas, for each walk. Ordinarily, the walks can be accomplished in a duration ranging from one and a half hours to two and a half hours at the maximum. I have also pointed out the highlights of each walk so that if you have less time you can finish in an hour or so.

QUTUB MINAR
COMPLEX

TO MEHRAULI VILLAGE

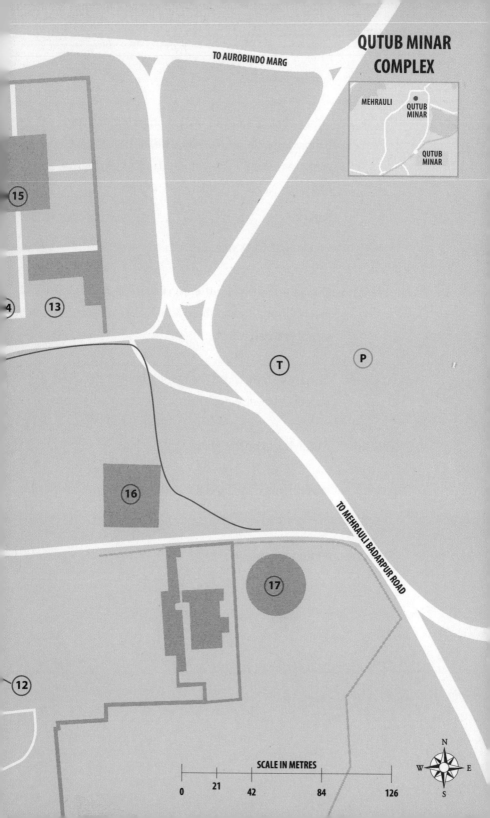

Timings: Sunrise to sunset.

Tickets: Citizens of India and SAARC countries (Afghanistan, Bangladesh, Bhutan, Maldives, Nepal, Pakistan and Sri Lanka) and BIMSTEC countries (Bangladesh, Bhutan, Myanmar, Nepal, Sri Lanka and Thailand)................ ₹10

Others: .... US$5 / ₹250

Children up to 15 years old............................... free

Highlights: Quwwat-ul-Islam Mosque, Iron Pillar, Iltutmish's Mosque Extension and Tomb, Qutub Minar, Alai Darwaza (best for an abbreviated walk).

Difficulty Level: An easy walk for most. The paths around the complex are paved and level. Wheelchair access to most buildings.

Metro Station: Qutub Minar on the Yellow Line, 1.5 kms.

Amenities: Washrooms, drinking water and small snacks available on site.

Parking: At the site.

LAL KOT

The Qutub Minar—a massive tower with a distinctive silhouette, is today the most readily recognized visual symbol of the city of Delhi. It is one of three sites in Delhi to receive the status of World Heritage site from UNESCO, and is one of the most visited tourist attractions of the city. Moreover, the historic, aesthetic and cultural importance of this structure and those immediately around it, more than justifies its reputation as an awe-inspiring place.

The Qutub Minar complex stands at the core of an early fortified city of Delhi—Lal Kot. This name literally means 'red fortress', due to the red bricks out of which the upper part of the walls is built. The lower part of the walls is built of stone rubble. Lal Kot was built about the middle of the eleventh century by Anangpal II of the Tomar dynasty. The Tomars were one of the many ruling clans of north India in the early medieval period that were collectively known as Rajputs.

In the middle of the twelfth century, the Tomars were overthrown by another Rajput dynasty—the Chauhans. Prithviraj Chauhan, also known as Rai Pithora, added considerably to the original Lal Kot. A new line of fortifications was built

towards the north and east of Lal Kot, which increased the earlier perimeter of 3.6 kms to about 8 kms. The resulting new fort came to be known after the king as Qila Rai Pithora.

In 1192 the Chauhans were overthrown by a new power in India, the Turks, who came from Central Asia. They were followers of Islam and brought to India an Islamicate culture and new techniques in building and ornamentation. From this time Delhi became the capital of a substantial kingdom and soon an empire, whereas under the Rajputs it had been at best a city of regional importance. Most of the remains seen within the Qutub Minar complex date from this early period of the history of Turkish rule, known as the Delhi Sultanate.

As one approaches the Qutub Minar complex the road climbs up to a slight rise, which tells us something important about the location of Lal Kot/Qila Rai Pithora. The site is a small rocky outcrop that is a part of the northern limits of a very old and eroded mountain range—the Aravalis. This location on a height was of strategic significance for the fort.

THE WALK

On entering the complex through the main entrance, you will notice many buildings all around. In this walk they will be covered in a more or less chronological order.

To begin with, go right up the path to the **Quwwat-ul-Islam Masjid (1)**. The name literally means the 'power of Islam mosque', but this name appears to be a much later one. It was originally known simply as the Jami Masjid or congregational mosque. This is one of the earliest mosques in India, the core of it built in 1192 on the orders of Qutub-uddin Aibak immediately after the conquest of Delhi. Aibak started out as the slave and general of Mohammad Ghori, the Turk ruler who conquered India, but in time became the independent ruler of Ghori's Indian territories.

This is a large congregational mosque, built over different phases. As you stand before the eastern doorway, look at some of its distinctive features. The structure of the arch itself is very interesting. It has the shape of an arch but not in its architectural form. A true arch consists of a number of stone blocks arranged in a semicircular formation so that the weight of the masonry above compresses each

'This fort was conquered and this Jami Masjid built in the year 587 (hijri) by the Amir, the great and glorious commander of the army, Qutubuddin Aibak Sultani, may God strengthen his helpers.' (Inscription on the lintel of the eastern gate of the mosque.)

stone against its neighbour and distributes the weight fairly equally between them. The arch of this doorway is different as it is built on trabeate principles. This means that the shape of an arch has been achieved by placing stones flat, one on top of the other, instead of side by side. Each stone projects out a little further than the one below it, until the gap at the top is closed. An arch made in this way is not as strong as a true arch and therefore the builders thought it prudent to add a lintel—a horizontal beam support, below the arch.

Before the establishment of the Delhi Sultanate, Indians had not used the arch in construction. Arcuate construction that is based on arch-making principles was first used by the Romans and then spread to West and Central Asia. The Turkish soldiers, newly arrived in Delhi, who commissioned the mosque, were familiar with arches in their homelands. It seems that they were able to tell Indian builders what the shape of an arch looked like, but could not explain its structural distinctiveness.

As you go through the doorway, look overhead and you will see the inside of a small dome. A proper dome would of course have been based on a true arch, so this one is not a true dome. It was built by stacking concentric rings of stones until the gap on the top was closed. The effect on the outside is of a wide conical shape rather than a proper round dome.

You will notice that you are now at one end of a large courtyard. This courtyard is the main body of the mosque. Around much of the perimeter runs a pillared colonnade. The pillars are mostly elaborately carved and on close inspection one can see many human, animal and divine figures. Such sculpture seems out of place within a mosque, since depiction of human or animal figures is unacceptable to orthodox Islam as being akin to idolatry. The answer to this mystery lies in the fact that these are reused materials from twenty-seven Hindu and Jain temples that had stood in the vicinity and were mostly destroyed by the invading Turks as an act of war.

Walking forward into the courtyard, you will see some graves here which are not inscribed but probably belong to some individuals who were associated with the mosque. A little further on, you will come to the **Iron Pillar (2),** which is the oldest structure in the complex. It dates from the fourth century and was erected to commemorate the victories of

Look out for the bright green parakeets that like to perch on the buildings.

2

Chandragupta II, one of the Gupta dynasty of kings who ruled over a major empire at the time. The pillar is made of very pure cast iron and is remarkable from a metallurgical point of view because it has continued to be virtually free of rust through the centuries.

Historians believe that the Iron Pillar was originally located somewhere else, as the original inscription talks of it being placed on top of a hill. One of the other inscriptions on the pillar dates from the eleventh century and refers to the Tomar king, Anangpal. A popular tradition associated with the pillar is to be found in the Rajasthani epic, *Prithviraj Raso*. This story is called the *Kili Dhili Katha* or 'the tale of the loose nail'. It says that Anangpal was told by a holy man that the pillar was driven into the hood of Vasuki, the serpent king, who supports the earth from below. It was also prophesied that Anangpal's kingdom would survive as long at the pillar remained firm in the ground. Anagpal unwisely insisted on uprooting the pillar to verify this truth, which resulted in the pillar permanently becoming loose or *dhili*. Simultaneously of course Anangpal's rule also became unstable. According to this story, the name of Delhi has its origins in the *dhili kili* or loose nail.

'By him, the king, ... having the name of Chandra and a beauty of countenance resembling the full moon ... this lofty standard of the divine Vishnu was set up.' (Inscription on the Iron Pillar.)

Just beyond the Iron Pillar at the western end of the court-yard, is a tall and imposing **screen of arches (3)**, most of which have fallen down. This screen is placed, facing west so as to indicate the direction of prayer that is in the direction of Mecca. The arches of this screen too are not true arches and this is the main reason for their collapse. Though the basic structure is built of rubble masonry, the surface of the

arches is decorated with beautifully carved sandstone in variegated colours. The pattern contains many interesting elements. There are inscriptions in the Naskh Arabic script, one of which tells us that this screen was built in 1198. Interwoven with the script is a design of naturalistic creepers bearing lotus buds. Towards the base of the structure you can see carved in stone the shape of a *kalash*, a Hindu ritual vessel. These decorative elements tell us that the Indian, mainly Hindu, workmen who executed the screen had considerable autonomy in incorporating their own ideas into their work.

It is best to orient yourself through the mosque which of course faces west. This will make it easier to navigate through the enclosure.

You can leave the main courtyard of the mosque through the north gate, which brings you to **Iltutmish's extension (4).** This part of the mosque, of which not much remains, was built in 1230 by Shamsuddin Iltutmish. Iltutmish was originally the slave of Qutubuddin Aibak and finally succeeded him as the Sultan of Delhi, and ruled from 1211 to 1236. If you look at the screen here, in scale and treatment it is quite similar to the one inside the courtyard though with an important difference, the motifs now are not naturalistic but stylized and geometrical. In the intervening three decades, the 'imported' elements of design had come to be better understood by the craftsmen creating the structure. It was a development that took place clearly between 1198, when the older part of the screen was built and when this part was constructed in 1230. At the same time however, the motifs of the lotus and the kalash were still used, and in fact, from now on became fairly constant features of Sultanate architecture.

Immediately north-west of this screen is the **tomb of Iltutmish (5)** built probably after the sultan's death in 1236, or possibly during his own lifetime. It consists of a square chamber that is open to the sky. A dome was probably never built because the builders, as has been noted before, were not confident enough to build a large dome without a proper understanding of arcuate principles. Inside, the surface of the walls is covered in sandstone, carved in a style similar to that of the screen placed outside. There is a profusion of carving but the juxtaposition of the various panels is confused and inharmonious. The western wall, which indicates the direction of prayer, has no opening and instead has a closed arch, richly decorated with carved marble. Just outside the northern doorway, one can see an opening in the ground, which leads down to the grave chamber. While the actual grave is in the ground beneath the tomb structure, in the middle of the chamber stands a large marble cenotaph.

Before leaving this part of the complex look to the north-east of Iltutmish's tomb. You will see a large circular structure built of stone rubble masonry. This is the **Alai Minar (6)**, built by the emperor, Alauddin Khalji, who ruled between

1296 and 1316. Around 1310, Alauddin commissioned a major expansion of the Quwwat-ul-Islam mosque. The colonnades of that expansion towards the north have now disappeared, except for the foundations, but the remains of a partly built enormous pillar can still be seen. This pillar was designed to be twice as big as the Qutub Minar but its construction was abandoned after the death of the emperor.

Going back to the tomb of Iltutmish, go through its southern doorway. A pathway leading through an open stretch will lead you to a group of plain but elegant buildings in grey stone. This is the **madrasa of Alauddin Khalji (7)** dating to the early fourteenth century. The buildings are constructed from dressed grey quartzite, without any decorative carving. Note the perfectly formed arches. The stones lining each arch lie side by side against each other, and a keystone at the top holds the structure together. It is evident that by this time Indian builders were familiar with the building of arches. The rooms are arranged in two wings, one running north to south, and the other running west to east. About halfway down the latter wing is a large room believed to be the **tomb of Alauddin (8)**, though no trace of a grave or cenotaph now remains in it.

9

From the madrasa one gets a good view of the most prominent building of the complex—**Qutub Minar (9)**. Minars or towers are frequently found attached to mosques and they serve to provide an elevated place from where the faithful can be called to prayer. Nominally this too is such a tower (called a maznah), but practically speaking, even if the muezzin had the breath left after climbing up to its top to give the azan or call to prayer, it would have been difficult to hear it. At 72.5 m high, the Qutub Minar is definitely overdone as a maznah. It is however a prominent and unmistakable political statement. It was consciously designed to be a symbol of the Turkish conquest of north India.

The first storey of the Qutub Minar was built during the reign of Qutubuddin Aibak (1206–11) and the rest under Iltutmish (1211–36). The name 'Qutub' suggests many different things. It could have been named after the revered sufi saint, Qutubuddin Bakhtiyar Kaki, who at this time lived in the vicinity. The word 'Qutub' literally means the Pole Star, around which the heavens revolve. This would also underline the importance of the structure and the new political power it stood for. Finally the name also brings to mind Qutubuddin Aibak, who commissioned it.

Decoration on the minar consists of finely carved sandstone and some marble. The tower is divided into five storeys, each of which is topped by a projecting balcony, the underside of which is richly carved. Bands of calligraphy encircle each storey and are embellished in the same style that is found on the screen of arches in the Quwwat-ul-Islam mosque. The inscriptions consist of verses from the Quran as well as the history of the construction and repairs of the structure. For instance on the fifth storey, there is a Persian inscription that reads, 'this minar was injured by lightning in the year 770 (hijri). By the Divine grace, Firoz Sultan, who is exalted by the favour of the most Holy, built this portion of the edifice with care. May the inscrutable Creator preserve it from all calamitites.' Also on the fifth storey there is a Nagri inscription giving the dates Samvat 1425 and 1426 and the name of Firoz Shah, and of Nana Salha, the architect.

The Qutub Minar has seen many rounds of repairs. Originally the tower consisted of only four storeys. Lightning struck it in 1368, damaging it. The ruling emperor, Firoz Shah Tughlaq, who is known to have repaired many other buildings around the city too, ordered it to be repaired. (He genuinely seems to have been interested in buildings for their own sake rather than as relics of previous rulers or dynasties.) In the process certain fundamental alterations were made to the structure. The fourth and final storey was

'The completion of this building was commanded by the king, who is helped from the heavens, Shamsul-haq-waddin Iltutmish-al-Qutbi.' (Inscription on the second storey of the Qutub Minar.)

15

'Lord of the kings of the world, the king of Darius-like splendour, the Sultan of perfect justice and abundant benevolence, the emperor whose orders are universally obeyed.' (Praises of Alauddin inscribed on the Alai Darwaza.)

rebuilt as two storeys and decorated using marble. Another round of repairs were executed in 1503 and both these events are recorded in the inscriptions on the minar. The artists, Thomas and William Daniell, who saw the tower in 1789, have depicted it with a small pavilion on top, which was destroyed some years later, probably by the earth-quake of 1803.

In the late 1820s, when Delhi was under the rule of the British East India Company, Major Smith, an army engineer was assigned to carry out repairs. Unfortunately many of the facing stones that had fallen down were put back without regard for the original order, so that the inscriptions became unreadable. Major Smith also added a balustrade in the Gothic style to the projecting balconies. It stands out as it is in a different shade of stone and of an incongruous design. A new structure was placed on top of the tower which was widely condemned and finally taken down in 1848.

To the south of the Qutub Minar, lies the colonnade that was a part of Iltutmish's extension to the mosque. The pillars here are not reused from earlier structures but were purpose-built. They are much plainer than the carved temple pillars in the core of the mosque.

Attached to the colonnade is a large red sandstone building which is known as the **Alai Darwaza (10)**, the gateway built by Alauddin Khalji in 1311. This gateway would have provided access to the mosque and minar from the south, where the population was concentrated at that time. The structure consists of a large square room with four arched doorways on each side, and covered by a large dome. The arches as well as the dome are perfectly formed. The surface decoration consists of carved marble and sandstone. The inscriptions are mainly praises of Alauddin Khalji, who is referred to, among other grandiose epithets, as a 'second Alexander'. The motifs are geometric and harmonious. A distinctive feature is the horseshoe-shaped arches with lotus buds forming a fringe along the edge. Only the northern arch is plainer than the others and of a different design. Another notable feature is the dome which has an opening in the top that is capped by another small white marble dome. The gateway represents a sophisticated stage in the coming together of indigenous and imported features to create a unique composite Medieval Indian style of architecture, often called Indo-Islamic.

11

Going through the eastern arch of the Alai Darwaza, you will come to the **tomb of Imam Zamin (11)**. Imam Zamin, who died in 1539, built this tomb in his lifetime. He probably held some important official position in connection with the congregational mosque, though not much is known about him. The tomb is in the form of a pavilion with stone lattice screens for walls. Polished white limestone plaster covers many of the surfaces of the building. The grave of Imam Zamin, which is within, is still revered.

12

Step out through the doorway which leads eastwards off the platform on which the tomb of Imam Zamin stands. Before you is a stretch of lawn, at one end of which stands the red sandstone structure known as **Major Smith's folly**

(12). When Major Smith carried out repairs to the Qutub Minar in the 1820s, he designed this pavilion and placed it on top. A wooden pergola in a Chinese style was placed over this, and over that was a flagstaff. The wooden portion was soon after destroyed by lightning and later this pavilion was removed and placed here, at some distance from the minar.

Go back to the main path and head towards the exit. Just past the steps and main information board of the complex, you will see a platform with graves and a small mosque. This late Mughal burial site has a number of graves scattered about the complex, some with attached wall mosques.

A little beyond, and to the left as you head to the exit, lies a **late Mughal sarai complex (13)**. The sarai complex and garden date from a time when the Quwwat-ul-Islam Masjid was no longer in use. It would originally have consisted of a large enclosure to house travellers, but

now only some of the buildings remain. The eastern gate of the enclosure, serves as the main gate to the Qutub Minar complex—note the scalloped edges of the arch that you would have walked under when you first entered. It is made of thin bricks typical of the late Mughal period, around the late eighteenth century. Running alongside this gate is a wall into which arched compartments are built. This arcade continues on the northern side. The western gate of the sarai stands opposite the eastern gate. Within the sarai there is also a **mosque (14)** of the same period and would have been built for the convenience of the travellers who used the sarai. It is built of rubble and plaster and is surmounted by three bulbous domes, typical of that period. It is still in use.

13

14

15

Attached to the northern wall of the sarai is an enclosed **late Mughal garden (15)**. The enclosing wall has at each corner a bastion surmounted by a domed chhatri or kiosk. Midway in the west wall there is a ruined pavilion. The garden itself has been considerably changed and is not representative of what the original Mughal garden would have been.

The capital of the empire had shifted far northwards (to what is now called, Old Delhi) and so had much of the population. But people still visited Mehrauli for recreation, for pilgrimage to the shrine of Qutubuddin Bakhtiyar Kaki or even while en route to the neighbouring town of Gurgaon. The sarai and its attached structures would have provided a convenient resting place among beautiful surroundings.

16

17

After you exit the main gate of the Qutub Minar complex, look towards your right. A little past the trees you will see a **stepped square structure (16)**, somewhat like a pyramid. Close to it is a similarly **circular stepped structure (17)**. These curious constructions date from the 1840s and were commissioned by Thomas Metcalfe, the highest British administrative official in Delhi at the time. He used to visit Mehrauli occasionally and lived in a tomb that he had converted into a home. He built these 'false ruins' as a picturesque addition to his view, in the typically English tradition of constructing 'follies' which were meant to resemble exotic ruins.

TUGHLAQABAD

7

6

MEHRAULI BADARP

SUR

3

SCALE IN METRES

0   21   42   63   126   252

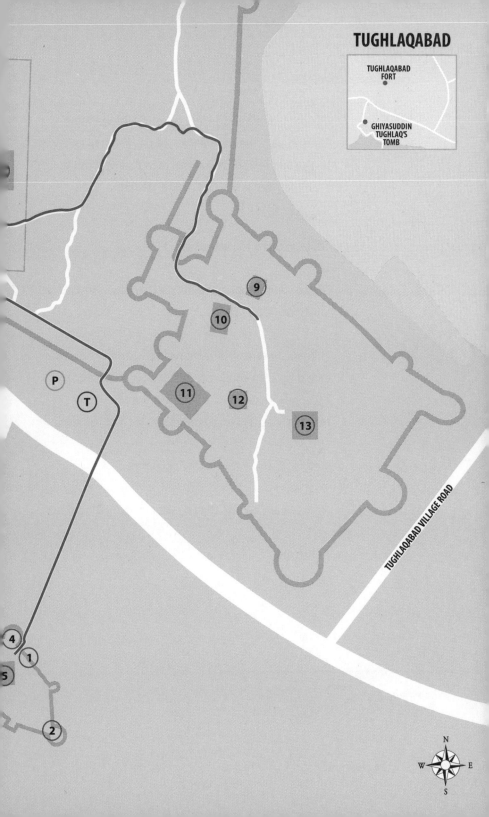

TUGHLAQABAD

TUGHLAQABAD FORT

GHIYASUDDIN TUGHLAQ'S TOMB

9

10

P

T

11

12

13

4

1

5

2

TUGHLAQABAD VILLAGE ROAD

N
W E
S

Timings:	Sunrise to sunset.
Tickets:	Citizens of India and SAARC countries (Afghanistan, Bangladesh, Bhutan, Maldives, Nepal, Pakistan and Sri Lanka) and BIMSTEC countries (Bangladesh, Bhutan, Myanmar, Nepal, Sri Lanka and Thailand) .... ₹5
	Others: .... US$2 / ₹100
	Children up to 15 years old .... free
Highlights:	Ghiyasuddin Tughlaq's tomb, palace ruins, Burj Mandal (for an abbreviated walk).
Difficulty Level:	There is considerable uneven ground inside the fort, including a few moderate inclines. Some areas may be covered with thorny bushes, so it is prudent to wear sensible footwear and garments that cover the legs.
Metro Station:	Tughlaqabad, on the Violet line, 4 kms.
Amenities:	None. Please be sure to carry your own drinking water .
Parking:	At the site.

FORT IN THE WILDERNESS

Tughlaqabad is a truly amazing place. The fortress walls are taller and more formidable than any other in Delhi. For a city that has more than its fair share of forts, this is saying something. When you enter the fort there are further walls, bastions and picturesque ruins of what was once an imperial capital city.

The context of this monumental construction is worth recounting. In the early years of the fourteenth century, the charismatic emperor, Alauddin Khalji, was on the throne of the Delhi-based Sultanate. He managed to not only extend the empire in the central and southern parts of India, but to fend off the Mongols who repeatedly attacked north India, on occasion coming right up to Delhi. In keeping the Mongols at bay, an important part was played by Alauddin's general Ghazi Malik, who had spent the major part of his career at the frontier, fighting the Mongols.

'One day as he stood before the Sultan Qutb-al-Din he said to him "O master of the world, it were fitting that a city should be built here." The Sultan replied to him ironically, "When you are Sultan, build it." It came to pass by the decree of God that he became Sultan, so he built it and called it by his own name.'
(Ibn Batuta, c1333–47)

The death of Alauddin in 1316 was followed by a period of turbulence for the Khalji dynasty. A series of weak rulers came to the throne and were unceremoniously dispatched in palace coups, until an individual called Khusro Khan usurped the throne and put to death all potential heirs of the Khaljis. Khusro Khan was not entirely popular and in 1320, Ghazi Malik who had managed to hold on to the province of Multan on his own, defeated him in battle. Historians of that time have recorded that after the defeat of Khusro Khan, since no Khalji heirs remained, the nobles decided to put Ghazi Malik on the throne, and he became emperor with the title Ghiyasuddin Tughlaq.

Though he ruled for a very short time, till his death in 1325, he managed to commission and probably see the completion of this massive project. The location of the fort, some 7 kms east of the earlier cities of Lal Kot and Siri, was entirely dictated by strategic concerns. To Ghiyasuddin the possibility of Mongol invasions was an ever present threat. And so this rocky outcrop was picked, surrounded by ravines on the north, east and west, and bounded on the south by a flat plain which could be turned into a vast lake by carefully blocking up the three rocky defiles further south.

The building of the fortress was not uncontroversial in its time. The emperor felt he was all-powerful and had no hesitation in ordering the entire labouring population of Delhi to devote their energies to this project. There were however important competing interests in Delhi. The revered and influential Sufi saint Nizamuddin Auliya was building a baoli or step well near his khanqah. Contrary to the ruler's orders, workmen continued to report for work at the saint's well clandestinely at night. Despite Ghiyasuddin's best efforts he could not do anything to harm the saint. When he heard of Nizamuddin's defiance, he was out on a military campaign and is said to have sent word back that he would punish Nizamuddin on his return. Though urged by his followers to leave the city, Nizamuddin simply said *'Dehli dur ast'* or 'Delhi is yet far'.

Sure enough, Ghiyasuddin did not enter the city alive—he was killed in an accident when a pavilion, constructed for his reception under the orders of his son Mohammad Tughlaq, collapsed. There were insinuations (reported by the traveller Ibn Batuta), that the collapse had been deliberately engineered by Mohammad who was in a hurry to be emperor. Moreover Mohammad was a devotee of Nizamuddin. In the course of this tussle Nizamuddin also cursed the new city of Tughlaqabad, saying, *'ya base gujar ya rahe ujad'* that translated means 'either it will be occupied by Gujars, (a semi-nomadic people), or it will be a wasteland.' Sure enough the fort was abandoned soon after Mohammad Tughlaq came to the throne and even today, a large part of it is a wilderness. The saint's prophecy, *'Dehli dur ast'*, is still a popular proverb which means something like— 'there's many a slip between the cup and the lip'.

THE WALK

After you have bought your ticket it is best to first visit the **tomb of Ghiyasuddin Tughlaq (1–5)** on the opposite side of the road. It is approached via a causeway that originally connected it to the fort but was broken to accommodate the road. You can see that you are walking towards a small and independent fortification. In fact this is also built on a natural rise in the ground. When Tughlaqabad was built it was felt that this spot too needed to be fortified to prevent an advancing enemy from occupying the height. Later, Ghiyasuddin Tughlaq decided to locate his own tomb there as well.

Look at the walls of the fort. There is a pronounced slope, which makes it difficult for intruders to lean ladders against the wall to scale its height. Towards the top there are rows of arrow-slits, which enable archers standing in tiers within the fort to discharge arrows to the outside. At the very top are a row of merlons, or kanguras as they are known in Persian. They too give an archer cover while still allowing him to shoot at the enemy. These kanguras, though picturesque, look a bit crude and is difficult to imagine how they could adequately shelter a man. As you enter through the **gate-way (1)**, notice that it leads to a passageway with sharp turns and twists, designed to slow down an advancing enemy.

In the roughly triangular space within, you might like to explore the edges of the enclosure first, which will give you time to admire the tomb from different angles too. At the narrow end of the triangle is a **bastion (2)** which has two openings in the floor. These are grain pits, intended to be stocked so as to last a siege. On the wall that encircles this spot note the ledge on which the archers could stand while shooting through the arrow-slits.

Make your way along the side of the triangle opposite to where you entered. There is a covered verandah all along the wall, and a little way down there is an opening in the floor, closed to the public, which leads to the grain pits. Further on there are two more similar-looking openings. Each of them leads to an underground passageway. One leads to the crypt under the main mausoleum, where the actual grave is located; the other goes similarly to a subsidiary mausoleum that will be described later.

3

At the end of the wall there is a fairly elaborate **pillared verandah (3)** which leads into a room that is open to the sky. This, along with other pillared verandahs positioned at various points against the enclosing wall, is believed to have housed a madrasa. It was not unusual to have an institution of learning attached to a tomb. There was a precedent in the case of Alauddin Khalji's tomb and was later repeated with Firoz Shah Tughlaq's tomb.

4

In the final corner of the triangle there is a **tomb chamber (4)** topped with a marble dome. Of the two graves within, the marble one in the centre belongs to a man; the other is a woman's. Notice how the small niches on the top let small

shafts of light into the room. The inscriptions over the doorways say that the person buried here is Zafar Khan, a successful general who conquered territory up to Lakhnauti, but died at a young age. It also says that the emperor Ghiyasuddin built this tomb, known as Dar-ul-Aman or 'abode of peace', for him. It is not clear from the historical records who this person was. Maybe the grave next to his is that of his wife.

Now come to the **main tomb (5)**, in the centre of the enclosure. You can see that this has sloping sides not unlike the walls of the

5

fortification. This however was not needed as a defensive device. In this case, it was simply an element of design that was quite common, particularly in Multan, where Ghiyas-uddin had spent much of his time. A perceptible slope on outer walls, known as 'batter', became a hallmark of Tughlaq architecture and can generally be taken to identify buildings from the time of the Tughlaq dynasty.

Another feature, which was to become a characteristic of Tughlaq buildings, is the plainness of the surfaces. There is minimal carving, though the expanses of good marble show that there certainly was no skimping on materials. The use of a lot of red sandstone and marble is however unusual for Tughlaq buildings, which tended to be finished in plaster. In the use of these decorative stones it is more like the

earlier Sultanate struc-tures such as Alauddin Khalji's Alai Darwaza at the Qutub Minar complex. Another point of similarity with that building is the lotus bud fringe along the inside of the entrance arches.

Even the mihrab is quite plain, and it is hard to say if it had some decoration origi-nally. Anyone visiting the tomb, who wished to pray for the peace of the soul of the occupant, would know which way to face. Many tombs therefore have this mihrab; as of course do all mosques.

The centrally-placed cenotaph inside is that of Ghiyasuddin. It is believed that the male tomb next to his is that of his son Mohammad Tughlaq, and the other that of Ghiyasuddin's wife, Makhduma Jahan. Mohammad Tughlaq is one of the most controversial figures in history. He has been criticized sharply by historians of his time as well as more recent historians for his revolutionary schemes, which failed gloriously, causing misery and chaos. One of these was the introduction of a token currency, an idea before its time. He is also reputed to have had a quick and cruel temper.

His cousin and successor, Firoz Shah, was a much milder man. In the memoirs of his reign it is recorded that he further embellished this tomb by installing sandalwood canopies over the graves and hanging curtains like the Kaba shrine from them. He also took measures towards some posthumous atonement on Mohammad's behalf. All the people who had been mutilated by the orders of the latter, or the heirs of those who had been killed, were approached. They were paid compensation and in return asked to sign deeds of forgiveness. These were then put in a box and buried at the head of the grave of Mohammad Tughlaq.

From the tomb enclosure, go back over the causeway, cross the road, and climb up to the main fortress of Tughlaqabad. You can see the wall stretching a long way on both sides. This southern wall is nearly 2.5 kms. The other three walls

'In spite of all his extraordinary liberality, the Sultan was far too free in shedding blood ... Every day there are brought to the audience hall hundreds of people, chained, pinioned, and fettered, and those who are for execution...those for torture...and those for being beaten.' (Ibn Batuta c1333–47)

are much shorter, creating a half-hexagonal shape. The total perimeter of the fort is almost 6.5 kms, and the wall in places rises more than twenty-five metres above the ground. The wall is punctuated by several bastions, curved outworks that provide a vantage point and cover for the wall itself.

As you enter through the gate you will get an idea of the vast size of the space within. This however is not the best point to get a bird's-eye view—you have to wait a bit for that. For now, turn left and walk along the wall for a bit. Notice the rooms that make up the bastions, from where archers could command a view of the surrounding area. You can climb up into them, and walk along the wall some distance. Climb back to ground level and continue.

You will soon come to a large **reservoir (6)**. It is built on the same principle as baolis or step wells, with steps leading down to the level of the water. At the top there was also provision for drawing the water up via a pulley—the stone supports can still be seen at the edge. The well/reservoir has no water now, and probably had little water at any time. Groundwater at such a height would have been difficult to reach, particularly in such stony ground. It might have been possible to store some rainwater, but maybe never enough.

Climb out and continue a bit further in the same direction. You will soon come to a broad, stone-paved carriageway that slopes down to another gate on the left. Don't take that, but get off the path and continue further. Just beyond is a slightly raised mound-shaped patch of land. Go up it

Keep a lookout for the wildlife inside the fort. There are birds, including the pretty green bee-eater, and nilgai or blue bull, a large blue-grey antelope-like creature.

6

7

but with care because the mouths of many deep pits dot the area. These, lined with stone walls, are most likely **grain pits (7)** for enough stock to withstand a siege. Grain is best stored away from light, damp and air, so these were the ideal storage.

8

Walk back the way you came till on your left you see some ruined buildings, extending quite a way inside the fort. These appear to be various **public buildings (8)**, and some of them were part of a palace with rather large grand halls. Pick your way through these ruins. One room has a pool sunk in the floor; another large hall has the remains of pillar bases. Along the top of some walls are brackets, which once supported a chhajja that has now disappeared. They are all built of stone and the surface plaster has in most places fallen off. Where it still exists it is quite black, but here and there you can see some incised ornamentation.

These buildings occupy a very large area and there always seems to be one more interesting structure looming ahead; explore as much as your energy and inclination will allow. The next destination is the high citadel to the east, past the gate through which you entered. Its large round bastions dominate the skyline in that direction. If you have gone quite far north in your explorations, you can approach it from the north too. When you get close you will walk up a formal pathway, probably designed for ceremonial processions by the emperor and his entourage. Alternately you can go back to the entrance gate, go past it, and up the steps to the citadel. This is the way the emperor would have entered after a trip out of the city.

The citadel was probably the more private living and working area for the emperor, and he went to the palace below only for public appearances and court. As you go

9

through the entrance within the walled citadel, on your left is a jumble of **ruins (9)**, mostly broken walls of small rooms. These date from the Mughal period, as is evident from certain typical architectural features such as cusped or scalloped arches and numerous small niches in the walls. This was evidently a small but reasonably prosperous settlement that grew up here long after the capital city of Tughlaqabad had been abandoned.

On the other side of the entrance to the citadel is a small **mosque (10)**. If your idea of a mosque is a grand, elaborately ornamented edifice, it is easy to miss this squat blackened building. It looks like a simple pillared verandah with arches, but if you stand facing it, you are facing Mecca, and nothing more is required of a mosque. It has certain stylistic features that mark it out as a Mughal building—notably its vaulted bangla or 'Bengal' roof, modelled on reed huts with curved

10

roofs found in rural Bengal. There was an inscription on the mosque, at least till the early nineteenth century, which attested to this mosque having been built by Sheikh Farid in 1618. Sheikh Farid was the bakshi or the paymaster of the army of the Mughal emperor Jahangir, and the founder of Faridabad.

From behind the mosque a path leads away to the south, to another large **reservoir (11)**. In size and construction this is comparable to the reservoir outside. It was probably thought prudent to supply the inner citadel with an independent water supply, just in case it ever had to hold out against forces outside.

11

Roughly parallel to the path leading from the mosque to the reservoir, and best accessed from near the mosque is long row of curious **underground chambers (12)** arranged on either side of a gallery. Though regular openings overhead let in air and light, it is infested with bats. It is too dark to really see into the rooms on either side of the gallery. It is possible that these were storerooms of some sort, or maybe since they were cool they were converted into living quarters during the hot weather.

13

If you choose not to enter the underground chambers you can take the path to the left which goes up to a building on a height, quite close to the row of chambers. If you go through the chambers you can access this from the other side. Climb up the steps and you will emerge on the flat top of a building known as **Burj Mandal (13)**, but which has also been referred to as Jahanuma or 'that which shows you the world'. The name is apt to an extent because this gives probably the best view of Tughlaqabad. Look back over the fortress. You will notice that the citadel you are within is a walled space set in the south-eastern corner of the fort. On your left, where you saw the palaces and grain pits, is another larger walled area. Both are in turn set within the much larger, walled city of Tughlaqabad. Much of it is green wilderness, and you can make out the long line of the wall that forms its limits. Close to the citadel, to its right, is a space covered with buildings. This is Tughlaqabad village, one of Delhi's many 'urban villages'.

To the south of Burj Mandal, against the outer wall is an easy-to-miss opening leading into a secret passage. Though it is not wise to try and explore it, excavations have revealed it to be complete with storage chambers and a disguised exit. Though many forts are reputed to have secret passages leading to other cities and forts, this is probably the only one that has definitely been found in Delhi.

SATPULA
AND
KHIRKI

KHIRKI MAIN ROAD

④ ③

②

SCALE IN METRES

0   25   50   100   SHOPPING MALLS

SAKE
COUR

SATPULA AND KHIRKI

PRESS ENCLAVE ROAD

1

Timings: Most buildings remain open through the day on all days of the week.

Tickets: No charge.

Difficulty Level: Most of the walking is on pavements with some uneven ground and steep steps leading to the top of the dam.

Metro Station: Malviya Nagar on the Yellow line, 1.5 kms.

Amenities: No facilities at the sites, though there are shops and large malls in the vicinity.

Parking: Parking is to be found across from the Pushpawati Singhania Hospital.

JAHANPANAH

The buildings in this area are mostly the remains of the four-teenth century city of Jahanpanah, founded by Mohammad Tughlaq. The Tughlaq dynasty came into power at a time when the Mongol Empire was a major threat to north India. The first Tughlaq emperor, Ghiyasuddin, had in fact spent most of his previous career as an army commander under the Khaljis, fighting against the Mongols, who on occasion came up as far as Delhi. Not surprisingly, a major project of Ghiyasuddin, even in his short reign from 1320–25, was the building of the imposing fortress of Tughlaqabad.

His son and successor, Mohammad (reigned 1324–51), while he expanded the empire further into south India, also perceived the Mongols as a shadow and a threat constantly looming over north India. When he came to the throne, the highest concentrations of population in Delhi were in the old fortified area of Lal Kot and Qila Rai Pithora, and in Siri, which had been fortified by Alauddin Khalji. In fact there was a considerable growth of population even outside the walls of these two areas, and the land between them had also become fairly populated. Mohammad Tughlaq felt it was wise

to enclose this area within defensible walls. He therefore ordered the construction of two lengths of wall connecting Qila Rai Pithora and Siri, and in the process enclosing the area between these two. This newly enclosed area was named Jahanpanah—'the refuge of the world'. Mohammad built within it a palace complex and a large congregational mosque.

The site that is covered in this walk is the area just within the southern wall of Jahanpanah. Though the wall has now

disappeared, its base can be discerned as a long low ridge of ground running parallel to Press Enclave road. At the western end of the road, where it runs into Aurobindo Marg, you can see the high wall of Qila Rai Pithora. Travelling eastwards on Press Enclave road, after a while the Qila Rai Pithora wall on your right comes to an end. Henceforth the foundation of the wall of Jahanpanah is on your left, but you will only be able to make it out as a raised area if you are on foot. The walk begins somewhat further east, on the same road but close to Pushpawati Singhania Hospital.

THE WALK

Along the line of the wall, and therefore just beside the road, you will see a large masonry structure. This is **Satpula dam (1)**, which was built across a stream that entered the wall of Jahanpanah at this point. You can see a stream of rather dirty water immediately to the east of the dam. This stream originally flowed under the dam. It was deliberately diverted sometime during British rule, to protect the dam from the effects of the water. One branch of the stream originates in the slightly hilly area to the south, another in the rocky area around Qila Rai Pithora. Just south of Niza-muddin it meets up with the Barah Pula nala which drains into the Yamuna river. In the fourteenth century the volume of the water in these channels was almost certainly much greater and cleaner.

In the 1340s, when Mohammad Tughlaq was building Jahanpanah, not only was Delhi threatened by the Mongols,

but a series of famines and plagues had caused discontent among the population. The need to protect habitation and agriculture within a defensive wall, as well as to provide an accessible and reliable source of water for irrigation was felt greatly. Both objec-tives were met by the

construction of Satpula. It allowed the entry of the stream into the walled area, so that its water could be used to irrigate the fields and orchards of the flat plain within. At the same time it needed to do this in a way that would not compromise the safety of the defensive wall by allowing intruders to enter along the same route. A closer look at the construction of the dam can tell us how this was done.

The lowest part of the dam consists of seven water tunnels that span the central part of the bed of the stream. A view of these can be had by clambering down a part of the sloping side of the dry bed on the side closest to the road. These seven tunnels give the structure its name—Sat (seven) pul (bridge). On either side are two more water tunnels spanning the shallower part of the stream. Climb out and go around the other side of the structure that is the inner part of the dam where there is a fairly broad terraced area. In the part immediately above the water tunnels you can see arches with grooves along the sides. This is where heavy sliding wooden boards would have fitted. A rope and pulley system operated from above would have been used to move them up and down. The main aim was probably to close the gap between the water and the wall. When the water level was low during dry seasons, the tunnels could have provided an easy entry into the walled city, unless the heavy wooden gates were lowered.

There were additional defensive features in the dam. On either side of the row of eleven water tunnels are solid-looking bastions. Inside each there is a circular room surrounded by smaller rooms which through strategically placed arrow-slits give a view of the dam and the bed of the stream. Guards would be stationed here round the clock to keep a watch for possible intruders. In this part of the building you can see some ornamental features too like the limestone plaster that covers the walls has been decoratively incised or carved.

From the sides of the bastions there are steps that lead up to the top. This will give you a good view of the surrounding topography. Along the narrow walkway that connects the two bastions you can also see the openings where the rope and pulley system for raising and lowering the sluice gates would have operated.

The water, which flowed from south to north, was slowed down by the dam and formed a pool just within. The water today is not clean but some of the original ambience can still be imagined. This beautiful spot was given an additional sanctity when the Sufi saint Nasiruddin Mahmud took up residence just north of this area in the fourteenth century. Nasiruddin was the disciple of Nizamuddin Auliya, and was the last of the great saints of the Chishti 'silsila' or order. He went by the title 'Chiragh-e-Dehli' or 'the lamp of Delhi', and his shrine and the area around it is still called Chiragh Delhi. It is said that Nasiruddin used the water of the pool at Satpula to perform his ritual ablutions just before prayer, and thus sanctified the water.

Jahanpanah was soon abandoned as a capital city, as Mohammad Tughlaq's successor, Firoz Shah, built a new capital at Firozabad called Firoz Shah Kotla. Satpula ceased to have a defensive importance, but it continued to be significant in its new role. For many centuries, the water of the pool was considered holy and was believed to cure many illnesses. Bathing in the water was also believed to protect against evil spirits. Till late into the nineteenth century, there used to be a big annual fair here just before Diwali, when people would come for a holy dip and even take some of the water away with them.

The rooms in the bastions were for some time also used as a school, giving the building an alternate name—the Madrasa. By the early twentieth century the Archaeological Survey of India took it upon itself to protect and conserve the building, at which time probably the local ritual practices and social functions associated with this building were stopped.

Climbing down from the dam, and leaving the building behind, turn right and walk along the main road. You will notice that the ground forms a ridge that runs parallel to the road. This is the remains of the wall. Soon you will come to Khirki village, and to your right you can glimpse a fort-like stone building set somewhat back from the road. This is the **Khirki mosque (2)**.

Khirki mosque is the most unusual mosque in Delhi and has some unique features. From the outside, the corner towers look like the bastions of a fort. The pillars on either side of each gateway remind one of the Qutub Minar (particularly those flanking the eastern entrance)—a fairly common device that was carried into later Lodi times. The heavy jalis of the windows give it a barred appearance. There is an overall suggestion of defensive architecture—and reminds us of how the Mongol invasions had coloured the view of the Tughlaq builders.

No date is to be found inscribed on the mosque or in histories of the period, so one has to make educated guesses about its possible date. It is most probable that a mosque of this size would have been built to serve a large population, which puts the date within the heyday of Jahanpanah. We do know that Mohammad Shah Tughlaq built a large congregational mosque, the Begampur mosque, in the heart of Jahanpanah, next to his own palace. He is not likely to have built another large mosque so close to the congregational mosque. It is therefore more likely that Khirki mosque was built in Firoz Shah's reign but when Jahanpanah was still flourishing. This was probably in the early 1350s or first few years of the emperor's reign, before the establishment of Firozabad.

The mosque is built in two storeys. The lower one consists of arched cells running all around the building. On three sides of the building— north, south and east, steps lead up to the second storey, which is the mosque proper. The entrance of the

mosque closest to the road is the southern one. Inside, the mosque continues to surprise. It is mostly filled with pillared arcades. There are just four open court-yards, occupying less than a fifth of the total area. Such an arrangement is unusual in India where the typical plan for a mosque is a large open courtyard. Drains slope away from the open court-yards to the edges of the building, to carry away rainwater entering the open court. There are carved brackets that support a chhajja all along the edge of the roof around the courtyard. The screen windows and the open courtyards let in some light, but the western side which is in the direction of Mecca and hence prayer, is entirely closed and therefore particularly gloomy.

In the north-eastern corner of the building the roof has fallen in as a result of a fire in the late eighteenth century. At that time the building was not functioning as a mosque. Those were politically troubled times in Delhi. The Mughal Empire was weak and the city and the surroundings were prey to marauding bandits. This led the popula-tions from the surrounding villages to take shelter within the solidly-built mosques and tombs of the older cities of Delhi. This happened also to Khirki mosque, which had long ceased to be used as a place of worship—probably when the Tughlaq dynasty came to an end in the early fifteenth century. In the middle of the nineteenth century, it was reported that 134 people and 147 head of cattle were living in the mosque. The north-western corner was used to store fodder that had earlier caught fire, which led to the damage. Sometime in the second half of the nineteenth century, the local British government ordered the inhabitants to be evicted from the mosque.

From near the eastern entrance steps lead to the roof. The sight here is spectacular, as the roof is covered with domes, arranged mostly in clusters of nine.

Leave the mosque by the southern entrance, turn right and walk around the perimeter of the enclosure to the northern side of the mosque. From near the northern entrance, take the narrow lane that goes off in a north-westerly direction. This will bring you to a junction of two vehicular roads. Go north on the road that runs north-south and is called Khirki Main road. Soon you will come to a fenced area on your right which contains some old buildings. The most prominent among these is the **tomb of Yusuf Qattal (3)**.

Yusuf Qattal was a Sufi saint who died in 1526–27. (The years are usually given according to the Hijri calender, and each year can overlap with two possible Gregorian years, unless the day and month are specified.) He probably lived in this area because he is believed to have performed ablutions at Satpula too. The tomb is an attractive structure. Notice the beautifully carved, red sandstone pillars and jalis. The design of the parapet around the roof is derived from kanguras. Here of course the merlon is only suggested in the very stylized design. Around the dome above there is a band decorated with blue tiles.

Inside is the grave of Yusuf Qattal that is still revered. On the western wall is the mihrab and on the panel above it the kalima or Islamic creed is written—'There is no God but Allah and Mohammad is his Prophet'. The script of this writing is the angular Kufic script, a particular variant of the Arabic script.

To the west of the tomb of Yusuf Qattal is a **mosque (4)** that was probably built at the same time. It has some nicely executed, though now discoloured plasterwork which is typical of the high quality incised plaster of the Lodi period. There are several other graves around these buildings, of persons now unknown. One of these is a ruined tomb to the south-east of Yusuf Qattal's tomb, which was originally a hexagonal pavilion, the roof of which has disappeared.

It appears that the tomb of Yusuf Qattal was built on a raised platform but the ground level of the surrounding area rose over the centuries through the deposition of silt brought by a stream in the area. The lower levels of some of these buildings, including the mosque, have been revealed recently when the earth was removed during conservation work.

HAUZ KHAS

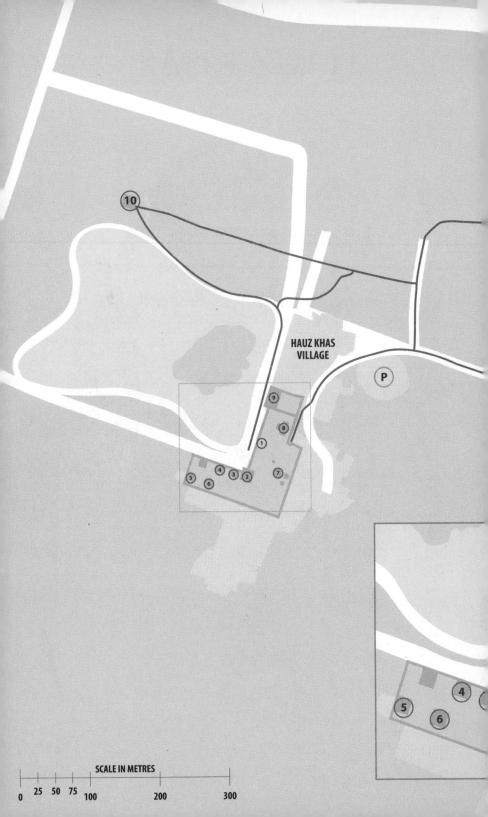

HAUZ KHAS
VILLAGE

P

SCALE IN METRES

0   25 50 75 100   200   300

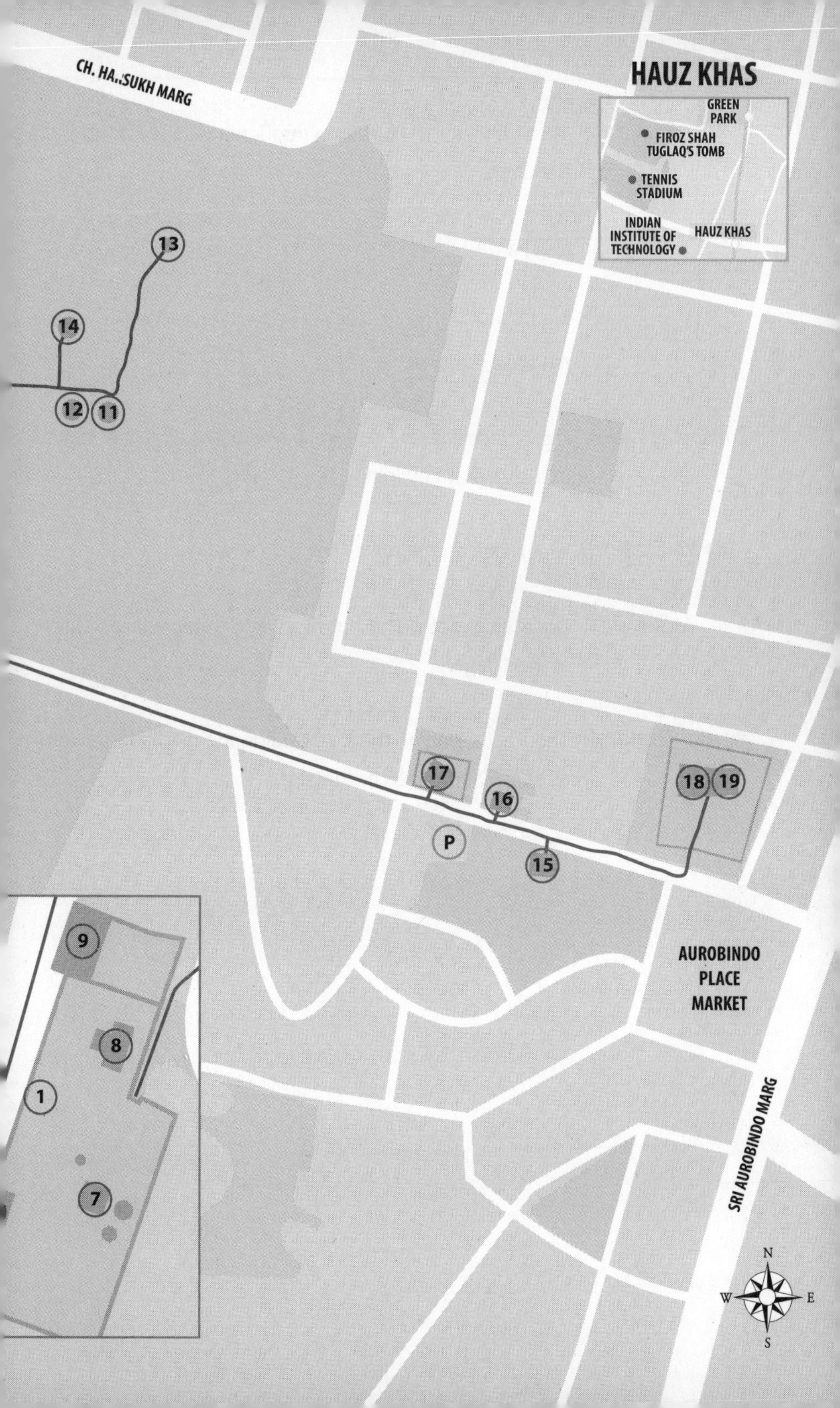

HAUZ KHAS

GREEN
PARK

● FIROZ SHAH
TUGLAQ'S TOMB

● TENNIS
STADIUM

INDIAN
INSTITUTE OF   HAUZ KHAS
TECHNOLOGY ●

13

14

12   11

17

P   16

15

18   19

AUROBINDO
PLACE
MARKET

9

8

1

7

SRI AUROBINDO MARG

N
W   E
S

Timings: Most buildings remain open through the day on all days of the week.

Tickets: No charge.

Highlights: For a shorter walk just see the buildings within the tomb-madrasa complex.

Difficulty Level: Most of the walk is over level paved paths. Flights of steps in the madrasa buildings.

Metro Station: Green Park on the Yellow line, 1.75 kms.

Amenities: No facilities at the site, but shops and restaurants aplenty in the village.

Parking: There is parking on the road leading to the village, as well as a DDA authorized parking lot.

ROYAL TANK AND COLLEGE

One of the first (and the most successful) of Delhi's 'urban villages' to reinvent itself as a commercial space with fashionable boutiques and restaurants is the Hauz Khas village that has a long history. In the thirteenth century, there was a large plain in this area, known by the name of Siri. This was where certain important battles were fought, notably towards the end of the thirteenth century against the Mongols by Alauddin Khalji. Though the major concentration of the population at the time was in Mehrauli around the Qutub Minar, orchards and cultivation were spreading northwards to Siri.

At the end of the thirteenth century, Alauddin Khalji decided to have a large reservoir constructed, to serve the needs of this growing population. The tank, known as Hauz Khas (the special tank) or Hauz-e-Alai (the tank of Alauddin) was spread over a huge area—some twenty-eight hectares. Monsoon water collected here in a large enough quantity to last till the following year.

Soon, in the early fourteenth century, the nearby camping ground of Siri (to the east of Hauz Khas) was fortified and declared as the new capital of the empire. The heads of

eight thousand defeated Mongols are said to have been buried in its foundations or built into the walls. Suitable buildings were constructed in it, including a magnificent palace known as 'Hazar Sutun' or 'thousand pillars'. In the middle of the sixteenth century, Sher Shah dismantled the building materials within Siri Fort for use in his city of Sher Garh (near the Purana Qila). Today only the remains of the outer walls of Siri, or Siri Fort are visible within which are the village of Shahpur Jat and the Asian Games Village.

After Alauddin Khalji, the focus shifted away from Siri as his dynasty collapsed and the Tughlaqs shifted the capital to Tughlaqabad and then Jahanpanah. The Hauz Khas too fell into disrepair, the water channels leading into it were silted up, and its dry bed began to be cultivated. In the middle of the fourteenth century Firoz Shah Tughlaq ascended the throne. In Firoz Shah's time the capital shifted further north, as the new city of Firozabad was built. However Firoz Shah had a great interest in setting up educational institutions, buildings, laying out gardens and commissioning water works. These were spread far and wide in Delhi and around. Among the many projects undertaken under direct orders of that emperor, the one at Hauz Khas was constructed in the 1350s and it combined all these characteristics. The tank was desilted so that it could again hold water. Along its eastern and southern edge a madrasa was built, and set amidst beautiful gardens. Firoz Shah in fact had such an attachment to this spot that he decided to build his own tomb in the midst of this college. Other people from the city also built houses along the banks of the reservoir.

This idyllic state did not last very long. Firoz Shah died in 1388 and the Tughlaq dynasty did not last long after that, beset by internal strife and the devastating invasion of Timur, or Tamerlane, in 1398. Once royal patronage for the madrasa was discontinued it soon ceased to function. The tank again got silted up. The surrounding buildings were abandoned. The area came to be inhabited by a rural population that grew into the Hauz Khas village. Some of the buildings were even used by the villagers to live in or to store fodder.

Much has changed around Hauz Khas from Firoz Shah's time, but it is still a charming place. The buildings are fascinating and picturesque and the tank once again has water. The surrounding parkland is green and teeming with bird-life, which incidentally includes migratory birds that visit the tank every year.

'The tank is filled by the rains in the rainy season, and it supplies the people of the city with water throughout the year. When I had pitched my camp here, the princes and amirs ... generals and officers, came to wait upon me to pay their respects.'
(Timur, 1398)

THE WALK

1

Begin the walk by going to the end of the main street of the village, where you will find a gate leading into the madrasa compound. Once inside the gate, turn right and you can walk up to the **eastern wing (1)** of the madrasa. If you climb up to the broad platform you can get a good view of the tank below. If from here you move to your left, you find yourself alongside the upper storey of the madrasa. It is raised slightly above the level of the garden and there is a long hall with pillars joining two rooms that have domes. On the inside, it has the look of typical functional Tughlaq architecture—built of solid quartzite beams and square pillars, with very little else by way of ornamentation. The pillared hall has an open plan looking out on the garden on one side and the tank on the other. There is evidence that some kind of protective grill work might have existed between the outer pillars.

It was clearly a beautiful setting to engage in scholarly pursuits and this was a prestigious institution of higher learning. A curriculum broadly based on a teaching of the Quran and Islamic law and jurisprudence was probably taught, along with mathematics, astronomy, medicine, grammar, rhetoric and calligraphy. It was a royal institution funded by the emperor himself, and so the best teachers were appointed, with probably a very good teacher-student ratio. Students received generous stipends, so in theory at least, economic background was not a bar to receiving a good education. If later traditions of the Indian system of education are anything to go by, an aspiring student would have had to convince his prospective teachers of his sincerity as well as ability.

The pillared hall leads into a domed room. This has a jharokha. Such jharokhas were a popular feature in indigenous Indian architecture from before the founding of the Delhi Sultanate. They became a popular feature of the composite style of architecture that evolved under the Sultanate. It combined elements peculiar to India, with imports like the arch and dome, brought in by Turkish immigrants. The Mughals later continued with the tradition of the composite style, with some modifications of their own. Another such element was the chhajja, which you can see along the wall overlooking the garden.

The domed room leads through a connecting passage to a much larger domed chamber. This is the **tomb of Firoz Shah (2)**. The inside of the room is finished in stucco or plaster which is decoratively incised and painted. The arches over the doorways and the squinch arches in the four corners are decorated with verses from the Quran. The drum, the circular band on which the dome rests, is inscribed with

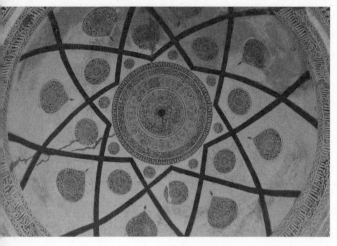

the ninety-nine names of Allah. The ceiling of the dome is particularly elaborate. The prominent motif is that of the eight-pointed star. The medallions between the lines of the star contain further verses from the Quran and the hadith (traditions or sayings of the Prophet Mohammad). All this decoration is in the form of incised and painted limestone plaster. The central marble cenotaph marks the grave of Firoz Shah, the other two marble cenotaphs are believed to be that of his son and grandson. Another unknown person is buried alongside.

To the south, a doorway leads into a small, paved yard surrounded by a stone railing. This kind of stone railing was another typically Indian feature that was enthusiastically adopted by Sultanate builders. On the outside the tomb wall has the distinctive slope of Tughlaq architecture called 'batter'. The inscription around the entrance arch tells us that repairs were carried out on this building in 1508 under the orders of the emperor Sikandar Lodi. It was fitting that Firoz Shah, who actually paid a lot of attention to the repair of pre-existing buildings including the Qutub Minar, should have had his own tomb repaired by a later emperor.

Today the exterior of the tomb has a cream limestone plaster finish. There are however accounts of travellers in the fourteenth century which suggest that the exterior surfaces of the tomb and the madrasa buildings were painted in different colours including red, with golden domes. Much of the exterior of the buildings of the madrasa is now quite blackened. This is because of the growth of fungus on the plaster surface, encouraged by various organic materials that were traditionally added to the plaster to make it strong, like pulses and the pulp of the bel fruit. The mortar, holding the stones together had an even richer mix of greens, cowdung and gur (jaggery), which made for a mixture that was strong but could also breathe.

Inside Firoz Shah's tomb you will notice that there is no qibla wall with a mihrab, the usual practice with tombs as well as mosques. Instead, in the west wall there is another opening into a passageway that leads into the **southern wing (3)** of the madrasa, mirroring the arrangement on the north of the tomb. There are identical domed buildings and a pillared hall. At the end of these you will find stairs that lead you to the lower level.

The lower storey, now much ruined, contains what was evidently the residential quarters for the students. Small narrow cells, with small openings for light and air and small shelves for storage, indicate a fairly Spartan lifestyle. Steps lead down from this area to the water, and are quite distinct from the broader steps leading down—in the style of a ghat, from the emperor's tomb.

Beyond the students' rooms is a **tall building with a dome (4)**. The room on the ground level has a flat roof, with a large and clumsy pillar in the middle for support. Narrow stairs built into the wall lead up to the upper level which has a domed roof and consequently a much more open look. This is in fact the great benefit that the invention of the dome conferred—it enabled the bridging of a wide space without the need to use intervening pillars for support, such as a flat roof made of beams would have needed. The precise functions of this building are not known but maybe one can find a clue.

If you emerge from it into the garden, you find yourself in what might have been a sort of entrance courtyard, of which the enclosing walls have disappeared. There are two buildings which now stand in the garden in front of this domed building which might have formed gatehouses. The **western gatehouse (5)** may have given access to this entrance courtyard, with the tall domed building serving as an impressive focus or even a reception area. From here one could move on to the **eastern gatehouse (6)** which led, via a small enclosed court, into the garden in front of Firoz Shah's tomb. The garden which ran in an L-shape all

around the madrasa and tomb buildings would have been a sight in itself, planted with colourful and scented flowers and fruiting and shady trees.

Within the garden you can see several graves and some **pillared tombs (7)**. Mainly in the form of open pavilions, the tombs are constructed of stone with decorative details in carved red sandstone. In particular, look at the decorative battlement pattern (kangura) along the edge of the roof and around the dome. There are no imposing cenotaphs; instead the site of the burial is marked by a shallow decorative indentation in the floor. It is probably the teachers of the madrasa who were buried in the garden, and it is not far-fetched to see their tombs doubling as open air areas for students to study in. (A possible reason for the flat floor unencumbered by a raised cenotaph.)

Two of the smaller pavilions have disproportionately heavy beams projecting out from under the dome, which has led

to a suggestion that they may have been connected as part of a larger building. They do not appear to be tombs.

This part of the garden is separate from another open space further to the north. Here you will see a large **T-shaped building (8)**. From its size and location, it is likely that this was an assembly hall of sorts, though it has been designated as a tomb in some books. The open pavilion structure was ideal for a public building, to make the most of the surrounding views and the fresh air.

On the other side of this building is the entrance to a section on the extreme north of the madrasa. Though in a ruined state, it is apparently a **mosque (9)**. Entering through the doorway, on your right is the eastern side which has some ruined chambers. The western side, which is on your left, is the qibla which in this mosque is an unusual one. Traditionally the qibla wall of a mosque would be denoted by mihrabs, the central one often larger and more elaborate than the others. Here the central mihrab takes the form of a jharokha with a flight of steps on either side leading down to the tank of water. The secondary

mihrabs are windows with jalis. Thus the faithful would be praying towards Mecca but in the process looking out over the tank which brought blessings in its own way into their lives—through water which they used for their everyday needs, for irrigating crops and gardens, and for providing a cool micro-climate; in sum, for life itself.

9

If any of the several flights of steps leading down to the water is accessible, you may like to go down to the level of the water now. Else, you will need to exit this complex and approach the water from the other side of the village. For this you must trace your steps out through the village, till you come to the entrance to the park which will be on your left, just across from the official parking lot. Enter the park and walk down for a bit and take the first turning to the left. You will soon come to a restaurant, and if you take the path to the left of the restaurant it will lead you, through a small gate, over a bridge, through a shady path and then up a slope to a mound with a ruined building on top.

'Because this madrasa is a monument of good works and benefaction, prayers, obligatory and superogatory, are constantly being offered within its precincts.' (Ziauddin Barani c1357)

10

There is considerable birdlife in the park, both in the wooded area and over the water. Look out for peafowl, barbets, hornbills, sunbirds, babblers, parakeets, red-wattled lapwings, hoopoes, and water birds like kingfishers, spot-billed ducks, pond herons, pochards and northern shovelers.

This is called the **Munda Gumbad (10)**, literally the 'headless dome'—reference no doubt to a domed, pillared pavilion on top of the building, which has since fallen down. This recreational building used to once stand on an island in the middle of the reservoir, which will give you some idea of the original extent of the tank. Now it is situated across the water from the madrasa buildings and from here if you go down and walk along the water's edge you can get a good view of the madrasa from below. You can see that to some extent the two wings of the madrasa are symmetrical—with the tomb of Firoz Shah, as the highest dome, forming the junction and focal point. Beside this on either side there would have been a pair of two lower domes separated by two levels of pillared halls—with trabeate or rectangular openings at the upper level and arched openings at the lower. Some of this has now fallen down, notably the second dome on the eastern wing. At the extreme ends the symmetry is somewhat lost. On the southern wing the vertical element is emphasized, with the tall, domed, two-storey building. At the extreme end of the eastern wing is the wide qibla wall of the mosque that projects a good deal beyond the line of the other buildings and has its distinctively large jharokha (the mihrab) at the top of the double flights of stairs.

Go back but not all the way back to the Munda Gumbad. Just a little past the mosque building, a few steps will lead you into the park and eventually to the bridge over which you came. Trace your way back past the restaurant, and when you come to the main path leading from the gate, turn left. You will soon come to a modern building and to

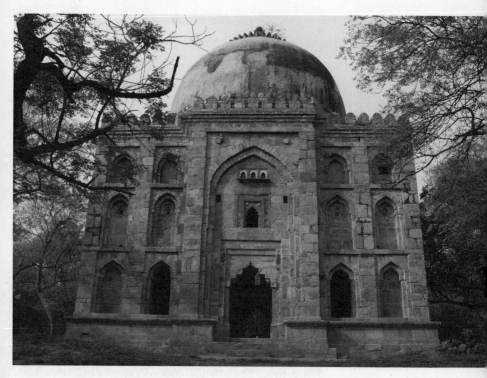

its right a path leads off into a wooded area. Take this path and walk till you come to a large, square, domed building.

This building at some point in its history acquired the name **Bagh-e-Alam ka Gumbad (11)** — the domed building in the Garden of Alam (Alam literally means 'the world' but it is also a man's name). It is in fact a tomb dating from the year 1501—a fact that is apparent from a Persian inscription on the outside of the western wall. Though the language of the inscription is not very clear, it seems to suggest that it was built over the remains of Miyan Shaikh Shihabuddin Taj Khan by one Abu Syed. Nothing is known of either of these persons.

The building however is a fine one, typical of Lodi period

architecture. On the outside are many arched niches, arranged in layers to suggest separate storeys, though inside there is only one large room. The use of neatly dressed quartzite with some marble, red sandstone and blue tiles for ornamentation has produced a beautiful effect. Inside, there is typical incised plasterwork, a closed mihrab on the western wall to indicate the qibla and several cenotaphs.

To the west of the tomb is a smallish **wall mosque (12)**, with a large number of graves before it. It was in fact quite common to build a wall mosque on one side of a burial. The mosque also dates from the Lodi period as is apparent from its style—the incised plaster decoration, particularly in the battlement pattern of the top and the delicate niches. It has rather distinctive bastions in the corners.

If you take the path that goes in a north-eastern direction from the Bagh-e-Alam Gumbad (orient yourself with the western wall of the tomb and mosque), you will soon come to the **Tohfewala Gumbad (13)**. This is probably a Tughlaq period tomb, much plainer than the previous one, but with large cenotaphs inside. On the way back to the park entrance, just past the Bagh-e-Alam Gumbad, there is another small tomb to your right, called **Kali Gumti (14)** ('black, domed building') because of the blackening of its exterior plaster. It also probably belongs to the Tughlaq period and is very plain.

When you exit the park and make your way out to the main road, just before you get to Aurobindo Marg, there are a few buildings on either side of the road that you may like to visit. On the right is a large, pillared, square tomb, known as **Barah Khamba (15)** literally 'twelve pillars', that belongs to the Tughlaq period, but is a tomb of some unknown person. Across the road from it are the **Sakri Gumti (16)** or 'the narrow, domed building' and the **Chhoti Gumti (17)** ('small, domed building'). The names are purely descriptive and from their construction, these buildings appear to be from the Lodi period. The latter is a tomb and the former might have been a gateway. The Chhoti Gumti has a red painted medallion in the centre of the domed ceiling.

A little further in a small green park on the same side of the road stand the two buildings known as **Dadi-Poti (18 & 19)** ('grandmother and grand-daughter') or **Biwi-Bandi**

18

19

('mistress and maid'). The names are entirely an imaginative construction, prompted by the fact that the buildings stand close to each other and one is clearly bigger than the other. The smaller one, Poti, with its plastered and battered walls may be from the Tughlaq or Syed period and has a distinctive lantern crowning the dome. Make it a point to go around to the back (the northern side)— the façade has some very beautiful incised plasterwork. It is quite unusual for the northern entrance to be marked out in this way as tombs are usually designed to be entered from the south, so that one enters closest to the feet of the person buried (the body being laid north-south with the head to the north). Neither does it appear that the other three sides have lost their original plaster.

The larger tomb, Dadi, is more typically Lodi, with arched niches arranged in rows. Look at the elaborate plan by which the corners of the square room are bridged by arches,

called squinch arches, to create a row of eight arched niches. The corners of these are then topped by short beams with carved brackets and then another row of beams until a sixteen-sided drum is produced and a circular dome can easily be constructed on it.

LODI GARDEN
AND
SAFDARJANG'S TOMB

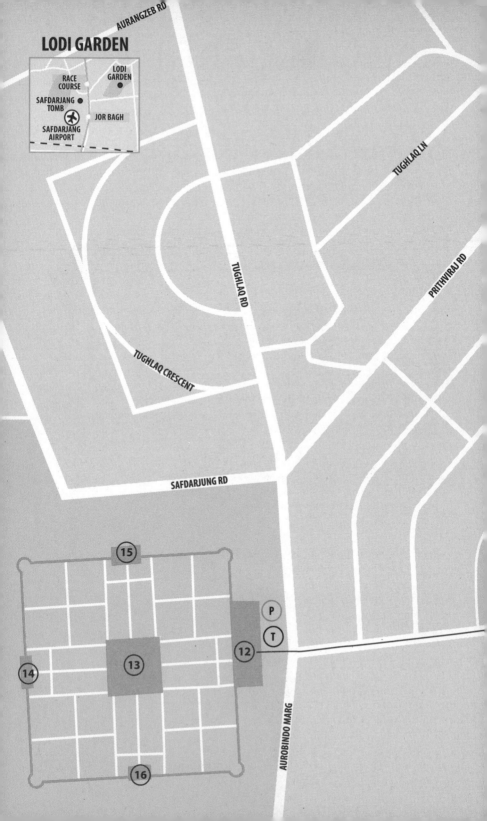

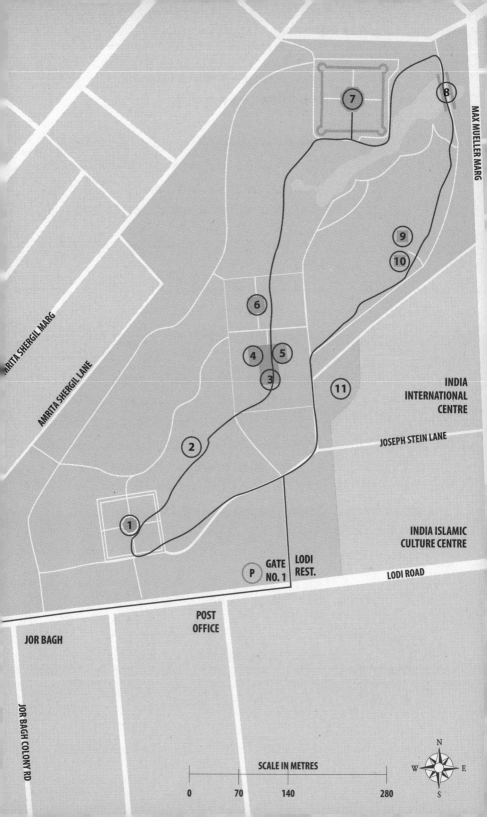

AMRITA SHERGIL MARG

AMRITA SHERGIL LANE

MAX MUELLER MARG

INDIA
INTERNATIONAL
CENTRE

JOSEPH STEIN LANE

INDIA ISLAMIC
CULTURE CENTRE

LODI
REST.

GATE
NO. 1

P

LODI ROAD

POST
OFFICE

JOR BAGH

JOR BAGH COLONY RD

7

8

9

10

6

4

5

3

11

2

1

SCALE IN METRES

0   70   140   280

N
W   E
S

Timings:	**Safdarjang's tomb:** Sunrise to sunset.
	Lodi Garden: Daylight hours.

Tickets: **Safdarjang's tomb:** Citizens of India and SAARC countries (Afghanistan, Bangladesh, Bhutan, Maldives, Nepal, Pakistan and Sri Lanka) and BIMSTEC countries (Bangladesh, Bhutan, Myanmar, Nepal, Sri Lanka and Thailand)..₹5

Others:...US$2 / ₹100

Children up to 15 years old..............................free

Lodi Garden: Entry free.

Highlights: Mohammad Shah's tomb, Bada Gumbad, Sheesh Gumbad, Sikandar Lodi's tomb (best for an abbreviated walk).

Difficulty Level: There are even paths through Lodi Garden and Safdarjang's Tomb though no wheelchair access to buildings.

Metro Station: Jor Bagh on the Yellow line, 1 km.

Amenities: Washrooms.

Parking: Near Gate no. 1 of Lodi Garden, and at Safdarjang's Tomb.

HISTORIC GARDEN

Lodi Garden is a large landscaped park in the heart of New Delhi. It is a green space with a wealth of natural and built heritage. This includes a considerable variety of trees and birds, and some buildings of great architectural and historical significance. In historical accounts we first come across this area as being referred to as Jod Bagh, as early as the thirteenth century. Since the word 'bagh' means garden, we can assume that this space was even then occupied by a garden, maybe with orchards. The name Jod Bagh lives on today in the area just south of the garden, known as Jor Bagh. This was a good location for a garden in medieval times because right through this area flowed a stream which was a tributary of the river Yamuna. The stream has long since dried up, but the bed is still discernable as a depression in the ground towards the north-east, part of which has been turned into an artificial water body.

From the middle of the fifteenth century to the beginning of the sixteenth century this area came to be chosen for the location of the tombs of some important personages, including emperors of the Syed and Lodi dynasties. Apart from the beautiful ambience of the place in the midst of gardens and beside a stream of water, the nearby shrine of the Sufi saint Nizamuddin Auliya might have influenced the choice of location. While the Syed and Lodi dynasties did not last long, the garden was still visited by many people over the sixteenth and seventeenth centuries. A possible reason was that it was next to the main road that ran from Mehrauli, an important suburb, to the capital which was at

Lodi garden is also worth visiting for its plant life. It contains a bonsai garden, a herb garden, a rose garden, a lily pond, and a butterfly conservatory.

Purana Qila and then at Shahjahanabad. Some construction activity took place here during that time too.

Lodi Garden attracts many birds. Look out for the black-rumped flameback woodpecker, brown-headed barbet, the common hoopoe, the white-throated kingfisher and the white kingfisher.

In the eighteenth century, with the decline of the Mughal Empire, Delhi and its surroundings became an insecure place. Plundering gangs raided isolated village communities at regular intervals. In these anarchic and unsettled times rural populations tended to take shelter within abandoned mosques and tombs. This happened to the buildings in Lodi Garden too, and a village called Khairpur came to be settled in it, with much of its population actually living within its buildings.

In the second decade of the twentieth century, this area received attention from the British government because it formed the edge of the site demarcated to form the new capital of the empire—New Delhi. During 1913–14 many of the buildings here were repaired. The village of Khairpur was obliterated and the villagers resettled, some in Kotla Mubarakpur and some in Punjab. By the mid 1930s, the whole space was landscaped into a garden and named Lady Willingdon Park, after the wife of the then Viceroy. Though the park was renamed Lodi Garden after Independence, the original name can still be found on a plaque outside the northern gate. In the 1960s the garden was re-landscaped.

Not far from Lodi Garden is the tomb of Safdarjang, set within large grounds of its own. It is most convenient to visit it at the same time as Lodi Garden.

THE WALK

Begin the walk at Gate no.1 of Lodi Garden which is situated on Lodi Road. Walk straight up the path and take the fork to the left. It will take you in a south-westerly direction, over a small bridge, to a large octagonal building which is the **tomb of Mohammad Shah Syed (1)**. Mohammad Shah was the third ruler of a short-lived and relatively insignificant dynasty of the Delhi Sultanate—the Syeds. They came to power in the early fifteenth century, the period after the invasion of Timur, also known as Tamerlane, when the Tughlaq dynasty crumbled and the former empire all but broke up. The Syeds consequently ruled over a shrunken and weakened empire. Due to their unstable tenure and straitened circumstances their building activities were fairly limited. The first ruler, Mubarak Shah, is buried in a fairly

grand tomb in the village of Kotla Mubarakpur (near South Extension). That was the site of Mubarakabad, a new city founded by Mubarak Shah.

The third ruler, Mohammad Shah, died in 1443–44 and is buried in Lodi Garden. The tomb is octagonal, a feature that is found in a fraction of Delhi's tombs. The single chamber of the tomb is surrounded by a pillared verandah composed of arches. The corners are supported and strengthened by buttresses— you will notice that each corner pillar extends outward at the base. The tomb has a large dome on top, surrounded by eight chhatris. One chhatri is placed in the centre of each side. The domes on the chhatris as well as the large central dome are crowned by lotuses.

The building is primarily built of neatly cut and assembled grey quartzite blocks. This locally mined stone is hard and quite difficult to carve. Such carving as there is, is therefore largely confined to some details that are picked out in red sandstone. Expensive stones such as marble were not used at all. The upper parts of the building are finished in limestone plaster, the original portions of which have now developed an aged patina. In places, such as the ceiling of the verandah, the plaster has been incised to create beautiful patterns.

The doorway leading to the inner chamber is of a characteristic design. A horizontal beam set below an arch forms a lintel. The resulting opening is framed by corbels made of red sandstone carved in a decorative pattern, reminiscent of Hindu temples. That impression is strengthened by the

The Syed rulers controlled very limited territories. It was derisively said of Shah Alam, the last ruler of the dynasty—'the kingship of Shah Alam—from Delhi to Palam'; Palam being where the Delhi airport is now located.

shape of a kalash that is carved into the doorposts. Such design elements were an integral part of Sultanate architecture which had evolved into a composite style, sometimes called Indo-Islamic. This included features that were part of a long Indian tradition as well as elements, such as the arch, that had been 'imported' when dynasties with original homelands in Central Asia had come to dominate Indian politics.

Inside, there are eight cenotaphs, the central one is probably that of Mohammad Shah and the rest belong to members of his family. The interior is decorated in incised stucco, which is made by cutting a thickly applied layer of limestone plaster while it is still workable. The patterns have also then been painted, mainly in blue and red. The ceiling is particularly elaborate. In the middle there is a large circular area of fine carving, surrounded by a large pattern of ribs painted in red. The western part of the domed ceiling has a smaller circular design. This serves to indicate the qibla.

Around the drum or base on which the dome rests, there are sixteen arched niches, four of which are open so that light can come in. These are not set right above the doorways, as one would expect, but off-centre. This is understandable if one remembers that right above the doorway, on the roof, is a chhatri that would block the light. The opening that most closely faces west (the qibla), is specially decorated in red sandstone. What would have been the doorway opening to the west is blocked with stone masonry, also to indicate the qibla. The outside surface of this closed opening is of decoratively carved red sandstone. It is likely that there was a decorated facing on the inside too, which has fallen off.

2

If you follow the path back to the fork and walk across the grass in a northerly direction you will see an imposing square building, with a large hemispherical dome on top. Before you go to it, walk across the lawn to your left, hidden behind some bamboo plants is a **mosque (2)** with a vaulted roof. It is quite plain and constructed of random rubble masonry, which essentially consists of rough stones held together with a strong mortar. The structure is covered in simply decorated plaster with an unusual red finish. Its style suggests that it was constructed in the eighteenth century.

3

Now proceed to the large domed building. This is the **Bada Gumbad (3)**, or 'big dome'. It is made entirely of dressed quartzite stone with some details in black and white marble

creating a nice effect. The façade consists of arches, most of them are closed niches but the others are open. The arches are placed at two levels which suggest a double-storeyed building. Steps on the western side take you inside through an ornately carved doorway. Before you enter look to your left. The adjoining building has a beautifully decorated jharokha. The back wall has a very ruined but an even more elaborate red sandstone projection. The jharokha was a popular feature of Sultanate and even Mughal architecture. At the corner of the same wall, which in fact belongs to the attached mosque, there is a buttress strongly reminiscent in design of the Qutub Minar!

Inside, the Bada Gumbad is a single large room rather than the two storeys as its exterior suggests. The surfaces are plain dressed stone with no signs of plaster. It is nevertheless attractive and its plainness enables us to appreciate the technique by which a circular dome was placed on a square room. The four corners of the room are surmounted by arches that match those over the entrances on the four sides. These are known as squinches and they are the means by which a four-sided room is transformed into an eight-sided one. Two additional rows of smaller arches transform this into a sixteen-sided structure and then a thirty-two-sided one. This produces a nearly circular shape on top of which the dome has conveniently been built.

The Bada Gumbad at first glance may be taken to be a tomb, but in fact there are no signs of a grave and it is simply a grand gateway. In size, proportions and even in some structural details it is not unlike the Alai Darwaza, located in the

Qutub Minar complex. What it is a gateway to, has to be guessed from the buildings that lie beyond.

A north-facing doorway takes one out of the Bada Gumbad into a courtyard. In the middle of this is a ruined platform that may have supported a chhatri and/or contained a grave. On your left is a small but spectacular mosque, commonly referred to as the **Bada Gumbad Mosque (4)**. It is lavishly decorated with carved stucco, both inside and out. Stylized foliage and geometric patterns along with calligraphy cover almost every surface. Most of the inscriptions consist of verses from the Quran. One inscription located on the west wall of the southernmost bay has been read differently by various historians but certainly gives us the date of construction of the building as 1494. In the days when this area was occupied by the village of Khairpur, this mosque was used as a cow shed.

Opposite the mosque on the other side of the courtyard is a much plainer building which has been called a **Majlis Khana (5)**, or an assembly room. It might have been used by those attached to the mosque as readers of the Quran.

Small rooms with shelving suggest living/working quarters.

Though the prevalent opinion is uncertain about the precise functions of this group of buildings, one prominent historian, Simon Digby, linked the Bada Gumbad and its associated buildings to the large tomb that lies immediately to their north, which is the **Sheesh Gumbad (6)**. This building is similar in size and shape to the Bada Gumbad but its ornamentation is somewhat different. There

are remains of glazed tiles (which explain the name which literally means 'glass dome') arranged in bands across the façade. It appears that the upper level was once entirely plastered and tiled because in contrast to the dressed stone on the lower level, its surface is rough and uneven. The chamber inside is plastered in a pattern quite like that of Mohammad Shah's tomb. The western wall contains a mihrab.

It was Simon Digby's opinion that the Sheesh Gumbad is the tomb of the founder of the Lodi dynasty, Bahlol Lodi. Bahlol Lodi became the Sultan of Delhi in 1451, after the end of the Syed dynasty. He died in 1488 and though many

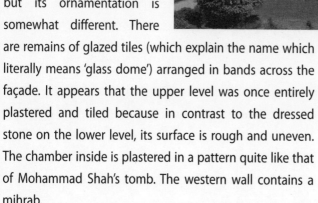

ascribe a modest tomb in Chiragh Delhi village to him, Digby demonstrated through various historical sources that Sheesh Gumbad is more likely to be Bahlol Lodi's tomb. He further conjectured, through a revised reading of the inscription on the Bada Gumbad Mosque, that that group of buildings was built around 1494 as an elaborate gateway to the tomb.

Interestingly the Sheesh Gumbad and the Bada Gumbad group are slightly out of alignment with each other. In fact the qibla wall of the Sheesh Gumbad is about fifteen degrees off from the true west. This defect was corrected in the later buildings, which according to Digby produced the misalignment between the two, and led to the prevalent impression that they were unconnected.

If you go northwards across the lawns towards the lake, you will come to a walled enclosure. This is a walled garden that contains the **tomb of Sikandar Lodi (7)**. Sikandar Lodi, who reigned from 1489–1517 was a fairly dynamic man who managed to at least consolidate the remaining territories of the Sultanate. He was also a patron of learning and litera- ture. Sikandar moved the capital of the Sultanate from Delhi to Sikandra, near Agra. Nevertheless he was buried in Delhi, probably to be near the burial places of his ancestors.

The entrance to the enclosure is through a large platform with two, ruined, square chhatris on it. On the inside you will see that the middle of the western side of the boundary wall is actually a wall mosque with a high central arch and a paved area in front. In the middle of the enclosure stands an octagonal tomb that looks very similar to Mohammad Shah's tomb except for the lack of chhatris around the dome.

Inside, the decoration is rather different. There is a considerable use of tilework, particularly framing the door arches and band of niches just below the dome. The western opening seems to have been blocked up at a later date but originally must have given a view of the wall mosque outside. Around the drum just below the dome, there are four off-centre openings similar to Mohammad Shah's tomb. This suggests that here too chhatris once existed on the roof or at least were planned.

When you come out of the garden, turn left and proceed along the wall towards the west and then north. You will

8

find that the lake is below you on the right. Soon through the trees you will be able to see a stone bridge over the water. This is in fact the best view of **Athpula (8)**, a bridge that you will finally approach in a somewhat roundabout manner by going out through one gate and in another. At this point in fact, you might like to view the north gate of the park from the outside. This dates from the time when the area was landscaped and named the Lady Willingdon Park.

You can re-enter the park now and go straight to the bridge. The term Athpula (according to some, Athpala) means eight piers, and the bridge in fact consists of eight supports spanned by arches. Some of these are hard to see as they are partly buried. The entire structure is made of stone and is a particularly attractive shape. The bridge dates from the time of Akbar who reigned from 1556–1605. It would then have been roughly on the way from Akbar's early capital at what is now Purana Qila, towards the south, where older cities and suburbs like Siri and Mehrauli were located.

9

10

Take the path that goes over the bridge southwards, this will take you back into Lodi Garden. In a short while you will see a couple of buildings to your right, which are attached to what was once a walled Mughal garden. The first one is a fairly damaged **gateway (9)** made of brick and plaster, with some attractive floral paintings over the entrance. The other one is a small **mosque (10)**, also made of brick and plaster. The attached garden has a modern layout, with probably little reference to the original Mughal plan. This enclosure might have served as a space for rest and recreation for those travelling on the road carried over the nearby bridge.

Continue along the path which will come out in view of Bada Gumbad. On your left you will see a small tower, which is probably the **corner turret (11)** of an enclosure wall that has disappeared. According to Simon Digby this enclosure may have encompassed the Bada Gumbad group of buildings together with the Sheesh Gumbad. You will now be quite close to the gate through which you entered Lodi Garden. Exit, turn right, and walk along Lodi Road towards **Safdarjang's Tomb (12–16)**. Safdarjang's tomb is located at one end of Lodi Road and it can be quite challenging to cross the intervening perpetually busy road which is Aurobindo Marg.

The tomb, built after Safdarjang's death in 1754, is the last grand mausoleum built in the classical Mughal style of placement within a char-bagh—a garden divided in a four-fold scheme. Safdarjang was the title of Mirza Muqim Abul-mansur Khan. He was a powerful man of his time, because he was not only the practically independent ruler of the principality of Awadh, but for a while was also the wazir or prime minister of the Mughal Empire. Though he died in Faizabad, his body was brought to Delhi for burial. This may have been because the family wanted to emphasize their connection to Delhi. The precise location may have been chosen for its proximity to the Dargah Shah Mardan, situated in nearby Aliganj that is in Jor Bagh. This was the shrine where a footprint of Ali, the son-in-law of the Prophet

Mohammad was preserved, and is particularly sacred to Shias, among whom were the nawabs of Awadh.

The tomb complex is entered through a **gateway (12)**, which is built mainly of brick and plaster. It is quite large and has several rooms built on two storeys on either side of the arched doorway. The ornamentation largely consists of moulded plaster and some striking painting, notably on the underside of the entrance arch. All the arches are cusped. On the right side of the gateway is a mosque which is not accessible to the public.

The gateway leads into a large garden, and in it, on a high platform, is **Safdarjang's Tomb (13)**. The exterior of this large square building is made of fawn and red sandstone, and marble. Some of the marble is said to have been taken from the tomb of Abdurrahim Khan-e-Khanan, located in the residential colony of Nizamuddin East. Interestingly, the marble has been rather unevenly applied to the dome. The dome is distinctly bulbous as it bulges out over a fairly constricted drum. This shape of the dome is one of the distinctly late

Mughal features that this building displays.

Inside there is one central chamber surrounded by eight others. The central chamber contains the elaborately carved white marble cenotaph of Safdarjang. Beneath, in a vault inaccessible to the public, lies the actual grave of Safdarjang and also that of his wife. The walls and ceiling are mainly finished in white limestone plaster, in high relief, highly polished and elaborately carved—another technique much used in the period towards the end of the Mughal Empire. The lower portions of the walls of the rooms are made of marble.

14

16

In the garden outside, built against the boundary wall are certain buildings quite similar to each other. The **Jangli Mahal (14)** or 'forest palace' on the west side, the **Moti Mahal (15)** or the 'pearl palace' on the north side, and the **Badshah Pasand (16)** or the 'king's favourite' to the south. You may approach them along paths leading from the tomb platform. These were arcaded pavilions meant to accommodate visitors. Now they have been enclosed and are used by the Archaeological Survey of India as office and storage space.

PURANA QILA

SHERSHAH ROAD

MATHURA ROAD

(1)

(8)

(T)

(2)

(P)

(9)

ZOOLOGICAL PARK

SUBRAMANIAM BHARTI MARG

PURANA QILA

JANPATH
PRAGATI
MAIDAN
INDRAPRASTHA
INDIA
GATE
PURANA
QILA
ZOO

③

⑤ ④

⑥

⑦

SCALE IN METRES

0   25   50   100   150   200

N
W   E
S

Timings: Sunrise to sunset.

Tickets: For **Khair-ul-Manazil** and **Lal Darwaza** free;

For **Purana Qila:** Citizens of India and SAARC countries (Afghanistan, Bangladesh, Bhutan, Maldives, Nepal, Pakistan and Sri Lanka) and BIMSTEC countries (Bangladesh, Bhutan, Myanmar, Nepal, Sri Lanka and Thailand) .... ₹5

Others: .... US$2 / ₹100

Children up to 15 years old .... free

Highlights: Qila-e-Kohna mosque, Sher Mandal, Khair-ul-Manazil, Lal Darwaza (best for an abbreviated walk).

Difficulty Level: Level paths link most of the buildings.

Metro Station: Pragati Maidan on the Blue line, 2 kms.

Amenities: Washrooms.

Parking: At the Zoological Park next door.

INDRAPRASTHA AND DINPANAH

The Purana Qila is an imposing fortress which was built in the sixteenth century. The raised piece of ground on which it was built however had a longer history of habitation. In popular tradition this is a site that is identified with the city of Indraprastha, built by the Pandavas, the five brothers who are the heroes of the great Indian epic, the Mahabharata. The first part of the Mahabharata, the *Adi Parva* tells the story of the clearing of the forest by the fire God Agni, assisted by Arjuna (one of the Pandavas) and Krishna (an incarnation of the God Vishnu). The second book, the *Sabha Parva,* describes the city which was then built on the cleared land beside the river Yamuna. It talks of palaces with golden pillars, decorated with precious stones, with pools of clear water.

None of the grand palaces described in the epic are visible within the fort walls, and it is likely that a fairly simple material culture existed at the time when the events related in the Mahabharata took place. Centuries of transmission of the epic by word of mouth led to an embellishment in the descriptions of the physical setting. This was the version that was recorded when the epic was finally written down. Excavations within the walls of the fort have revealed ancient habitation, which tells us that people lived at this site perhaps as far back as 1000 BC, the time when the events mentioned in the Mahabharata are believed to have taken place.

'Jumna's dark and limpid waters laved Yudhishthir's palace walls; And to hail him Dharma-raja, monarchs thronged his royal halls.' (R.C. Dutt, *The Mahabharata in English Verse*, 1899)

97

'... all the great mushaikhs (religious men), the respectable saiyids, the learned persons and all the elders of the city of Delhi, accompanied the King ... to the spot. His Majesty with his holy hand put a brick on the earth, and then each person from that concourse of great men put a stone on the ground.'
(Khondamir, *Humayun-nama*, 1534)

The Mahabharata also talks of the later abandonment of this capital city by the Pandavas. Archaeological evidence tells us that some habitation continued to exist here over the following centuries. In 1533, the second Mughal emperor Humayun began at this site the construction of a fortified city called Dinpanah, 'the asylum of the faith'. Within a year the outer walls, bastions and gates were complete. Humayun's reign was rudely interrupted in 1540 by Sher Shah Sur, who became the ruler at Delhi, forcing Humayun into exile.

Sher Shah in his turn established an extensive city stretching from Dinpanah northwards to the fourteenth century city of Firozabad. Not much of this city remains; the building materials were probably utilized in later constructions such as the city of Shahjahanabad in the seventeenth century. Then in the twentieth century the British imperial city of New Delhi was built over the site.

Humayun returned to the throne in 1555 after defeating one of Sher Shah's successors, but died in an accident a few months later. He was succeeded by his thirteen-year-old son Akbar. After some years of ruling from Delhi, Akbar moved his capital to Agra and after a while Purana Qila came to be occupied by the village of Indarpat—recalling the old name of Indraprastha. The village was cleared in the early twentieth century by the Archaeological Survey of India which then conserved the buildings and turned the fort into a tourist attraction. There was an interregnum in 1947–48 when the country was partitioned, and the fort for a while became a refugee camp holding mainly Muslims escaping the rioting and waiting for migration to the newly-created nation of Pakistan.

THE WALK

The imposing walls of the fort can best be seen on the eastern side by walking along a path that leads off to the left just before you get to the ticket window. The walls are high and straight, crowned by battlements and two rows of arrow/gun-slits. The moat that once ran around much of the perimeter of the fort has now been turned into a water body. The river Yamuna once lapped against the eastern edge of the fort, but has long since changed its course eastwards.

The northern side of the fort has a tall gateway called the **Talaqi Darwaza (1)** or the 'forbidden gate'. It is not quite certain when and why this name was given to it. The commonly told story is that a certain king went out to battle through it, vowing not to re-enter unless victorious, but as he died in battle, the gate was shut for ever. This account cannot be correlated to any of the historic events connected with the Purana Qila and thus has to be put down to inventive tourist guides.

The gateway itself is quite interesting. It is quite tall and actually has two doorways through it, set one on top of the other. It seems that the lower one was at the level of the water in the moat, and it was the upper one, certainly far more ornamental, that was the main entrance. Its level suggests that there must have been a drawbridge or a causeway leading to it from across the moat. The upper part of the gateway has two beautifully-carved red sandstone jharokhas on either side of the arched doorway. Above each jharokha is a square panel with a carved figure of a leogryph, a mythical lion-like creature, fighting a man. This typically Buddhist motif is a surprise in such a location, particularly as buildings commissioned by Muslim patrons normally did not feature human or animal figures. Such depictions could be interpreted as idolatry, which is anathema to Islam. The presence of such a motif points to the broadminded and eclectic approach of builders of this fort. The gate is topped by three chhatris or pillared kiosks, with some remnants of blue tilework on them.

The main entry into the fort now is through the **Bada Darwaza (2)** or the 'large gate'. It is in fact not as tall as the Talaqi Darwaza, nor as ornate, and it has only one arched entrance. In style though it is similar, with red sandstone facing and inlays in white and black marble providing a nice contrast. This gate too has decorative jharokhas, and above them a row of arrow-slits. The six-pointed star, here placed on either side of the arch, is a cosmic symbol and a fairly commonly used motif in Mughal architecture.

There are two bastions on either side of the gate, and the one on your left would have originally had the same kind of chhatri that you see on top of the one on the right. The bastion on the right also has the battlements on top fairly intact—these consist of the parapet with kanguras on top. The kanguras along the rest of the wall have disappeared.

As you pass through the gate to the inside, you will notice that it has quite a few cell-like chambers arranged on different levels. The gate is quite damaged and the structure immediately surrounding the arch at the entrance was probably built during repair work carried out in the early twentieth century.

The path leading from the gate intersects with another, on which if you turn left, you can go to the inside of the Talaqi Darwaza. This too is in ruins but you can see the remains of some incised plaster work high up on the walls. If instead you continue straight, you will come to the most spectacular building within the fort—the **Qila-e-Kohna Masjid (3)**. The name literally means 'the mosque of the old fort'.

3

There is some controversy as to whether the mosque was built by Humayun, or by Sher Shah. None of the inscriptions tells us either the date or the name of the patron. In any event this remarkable building displays a range of decorative techniques. The mosque is essentially built in the grey quartzite that is locally mined, but there is a lavish use of red and yellow sandstone and white and black marble. Decorative techniques include stone intarsia or inlay work, beautiful stone carving and some tile work too. As you approach you will see the back of the mosque, which has some projecting jharokhas. It also has two pillars set against the wall, which remind one of the Qutub Minar. Along the top of the wall is a row of stylized kanguras. These of course would not have served the defensive function of true battlements as they are too small and placed on the roof of a mosque that is otherwise open. They are simply a decorative feature. Look closely at the prominent red sandstone turrets at either end of this back wall. The lowest level has niches framed by beautifully carved corbels.

Come around to face the façade of the mosque. There are interesting motifs that have been used in its ornamentation. The base of the slender pillars on either side of the three central arches is carved in the shape of a kalash. The use of this motif was quite prevalent in the architecture of the Islamic rulers of India, and represents the evolution of a composite cultural style. The other distinctly Indian motif that was used extensively was the lotus. Here you can see a fringe of lotus buds along the inside of the arches. There is also a large stylized lotus capping the top of the dome, in turn crowned by a finial on the pattern commonly found on Hindu temples. The lotus also appears in the form of bosses or raised medallions on various surfaces in the building. The arches at either end are simple in design but the bases, carved in red sandstone, have a Chaitya window pattern frequently used in Buddhist art and architecture.

If you stand facing the arches of the mosque you are facing Mecca, which is to the west. This is the direction of prayer for Muslims, and if you enter through the arches you will see that there are mihrabs along the qibla wall. The mihrabs are richly decorated with carved and inlaid marble, but again note the kalash-shaped pillar bases and the lotus rosettes. There are bands of Arabic calligraphy, mainly verses from the Quran. The other walls are profusely decorated too. An attractive feature is the black and white marble niches made in the wall to keep lamps.

In this building you can see two methods by which a square space was surmounted by a circular dome. In the central bay, the corners of the room are capped by arches, called squinch arches, constructed in quartzite. These help to create a band of eight arches and these in turn are topped by sixteen smaller arches that produces a shape that is

nearly circular. Incidentally, this band of arches at the base of the dome is decorated with ceramic tiles. In the bays on either side of the central one, the approach is different. Here the space at the corners of the squares is filled in by horizontal or trabeate supports which are then beautifully carved. The dome on top is very shallow. The bays at the extreme ends are rectangular and their ceilings have a very complex construction.

South of the Qila-e-Kohna is a two-storeyed octagonal building known as **Sher Mandal (4)**. Though its name suggests that this was built by Sher Shah, it may have been Humayun who actually had this constructed. Sher Mandal is a name familiar in history as a palace built by Sher Shah, though it is not at all certain that this was that building, most probably not. On the other hand, in style this building is quite similar to some Mughal pavilions described in historical accounts or seen in illustrations of that period. It certainly does not look like a palace. Access to the upper floors of the building is not open to the public and the lowest level is actually solid except for a staircase going up. The white marble inlay on the red sandstone is fairly simple compared to the intricacy at the mosque, but quite attractive. The building is topped by a chhatri.

Sher Mandal has an interesting story attached to it. On 20 January 1556, a few months after Humayun had recaptured the throne of Delhi, he climbed up to the roof of this building, which incidentally he seems to have been using as a library and astronomical observatory. He acknowledged the people who had gathered at the nearby mosque and busied himself in making preparations for some astronomical observations. Suddenly he heard the call to prayer, and in a hurry to either come downstairs or to kneel, he tripped over his long robe and tumbled down stairs. Four days later he died of his injuries, at fifty-one.

Somewhat to the north-west of Sher Mandal is a **baoli (5)** closed off by a metal railing. A long and rather narrow stepped passageway leads down to the water level. Baolis were designed to allow easy access to the water via steps, though usually there was also a conventional well at the back where water could be drawn up in a bucket.

To the south of Sher Mandal is a brickwork structure, the **hammam (6)**. Its ruined state makes it difficult to reconstruct what it must have looked like but you can see the remains of terracotta pipes, water chutes and brick-work chambers.

Further south, at the extreme end of the path that leads from the Talaqi Darwaza, is the **Humayun Darwaza (7)**, the third entrance into the fort. From the inside, broad steps lead down to the lower part of the gate, which like the other gates has several chambers arranged at different levels. The decorative part of the gate is actually on the outside, and

can be seen from the Zoological Park. It is similar to the Talaqi Darwaza. One point of difference is that it still has a few sandstone covered merlons, which have disappeared from the other gates. In the panels above the two jharokhas are two finely-carved, small, marble elephants. Though its name suggests that it was built by Humayun, some historians believe, on the basis of an inscription in ink which was found in one of the rooms, that it was built during Sher Shah's reign.

On your way out of the fort you might like to visit the archaeological museum located near the Bada Darwaza. It has artefacts from different eras in Delhi's history, particularly finds such as pottery and other everyday objects unearthed in excavations in Purana Qila and elsewhere, for instance at Lal Kot.

Across the road from the Purana Qila are two further buildings of interest. One is the **Lal Darwaza (8)**, an impressive grey quartzite and red sandstone gateway. It is approached via a broad path on either side of which are arcades that might have contained shops. Attached to either side of the gate are battlemented walls and bastions, suggesting that this was the southern limit of a walled city, almost certainly the Sher Garh founded by Sher Shah Sur. The northern limit of this city is to be found some 3 kms north, at the gateway known as Khuni Darwaza, located near Firoz Shah Kotla.

The Lal Darwaza is in a ruined state but you can still see some remains of ornamentation. There are jharokhas, white and black marble inlay, lotus rosettes, and some tile work. The battlements along the top of the gate and wall consist of arrow/gun-slits and kanguras.

Not far from the Lal Darwaza, just beside the road is the building known as **Khair-ul-Manazil (9)**. This is a mosque and madrasa complex built by Maham Angah, the wet nurse of the emperor Akbar. The wet nurses were still an important influence in Akbar's life and in the court as he was only thirteen years old when he became emperor. Maham Angah commissioned this building to house a mosque and an educational institution, in 1561–62, the early part of Akbar's reign.

The gateway is fairly plain-looking and inside, the building is rather the worse for wear. Across the courtyard, facing the gateway is the main part of the mosque. An inscription over the central arch tells us name of the building, the year of its construction and the name of its patron. There are some remains of the attractive tile work and incised plaster that was used in decorating the walls. The rooms arranged around the other sides of the courtyard on two levels would have housed the college or madrasa.

We learn from one of the histories written during Akbar's reign, that this was the scene of an attempt on the life of the emperor. One day, in 1564, while returning from a hunting expedition, Akbar was passing through the bazaar of Delhi, presumably the street in front of Lal Darwaza, when a man standing on the roof of the madrasa shot an arrow at him, which luckily only grazed the skin. The would-be assassin was immediately caught and put to death.

NIZAMUDDIN

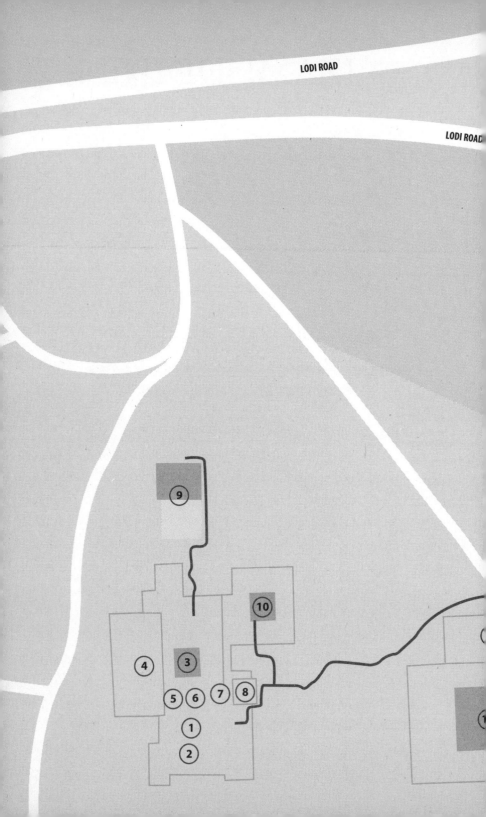

LODI ROAD

LODI ROAD

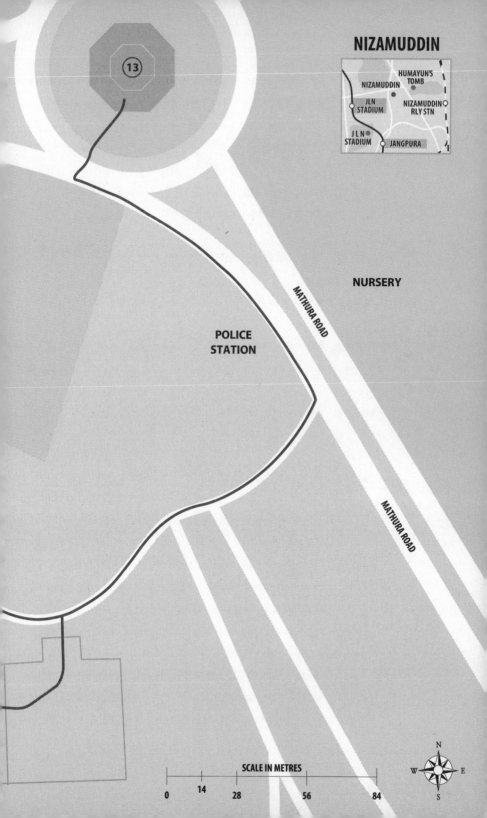

NIZAMUDDIN

HUMAYUN'S
TOMB
NIZAMUDDIN
JLN
STADIUM
NIZAMUDDIN
RLY STN
JLN
STADIUM
JANGPURA

(13)

NURSERY

MATHURA ROAD

POLICE
STATION

MATHURA ROAD

SCALE IN METRES

0   14   28   56   84

N
W   E
S

Timings: Most buildings remain open through the day on all days of the week.

Tickets: No charge.

Highlights: All the buildings in the dargah enclosure and Atgah Khan's tomb and Chaunsath Khamba.

Difficulty Level: Reasonably level paths through the basti.

Metro Station: Jawaharlal Nehru Stadium on the Violet line, 1 km.

Amenities: None on site. The basti has some famous eating places like Karims and Aap ki Khatir.

Parking: On the street in Nizamuddin West or at Humayun's tomb across Mathura Road.

Special Tip: It is customary to cover the head when going into the shrine itself. It is also better to avoid wearing shorts or short skirts and sleeveless garments.

Events: Thursday is the special day for visits to the shrine as in the evening you can hear Qawwali—devotional singing particularly associated with the Sufi dargah. Other days associated with festivities are the two 'Urs' of Nizamuddin Auliya and of Amir Khusro. The Urs, literally 'wedding' is the anniversary of the death of the saint, signifying his union with God. In addition, the Hindu festival of Basant Panchmi is celebrated as Basant (spring) in the dargah.

HISTORIC BASTI

Nizamuddin is a name which many associate simply with a posh residential area in central Delhi, or with the major railway station located there. The locality, in fact, gets its name from one of the major Sufi saints of Delhi, Nizamuddin Auliya, whose burial place is one of the most revered shrines in India and an important centre of pilgrimage.

Mohammad Nizamuddin was born in 1235 in Badaun (in the state of Uttar Pradesh), to a family with a background of learning and piety. He lost his father at a young age and while still a youth, came to Delhi with his mother. His early years in Delhi were spent in scholarly pursuits, but were also marked by the death of his mother. Though his initial ambition was to become a qazi or a jurist—he started spending a lot of time in the company of men who were Sufis, or Islamic mystics. In particular he found himself being mysteriously drawn to a great Sufi of the time— Fariduddin Ganj-e-Shakar, who lived in Ajodhan (now in Pakistan) and of whom Nizamuddin only knew by reputation. At the age of twenty, he had a mystical experience, and his soul was illuminated with the love of God that replaced

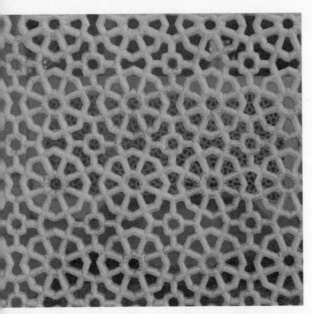

all worldliness. He set out for Ajodhan to meet Fariduddin Ganj-e-Shakar, who was the direct spiritual successor of the great saint, Qutubuddin Bakhtiyar Kaki. The Sufi received Nizamuddin and eventually appointed him as his spiritual successor.

Nizamuddin returned to Delhi and began to live in the locality of Ghiyaspur or present day Nizamuddin. He soon acquired a large following, which included the emperors Alauddin Khalji and Mohammad Tughlaq, and powerful courtiers like Amir Khusro. He was buried close to where he had lived, and his grave became an important place of pilgrimage and the centre of a bustling settlement or the 'basti'. Many burials have also taken place down the centuries in the vicinity of the saint's grave, in a wide radius that extends to the tombs of the Mughal emperor, Humayun and the poet and soldier Rahim. As a result, this is an area rich in buildings and stories.

The immediate surroundings of the dargah are a warren of narrow lanes. Many of the people living here have done so for many generations and are connected to the shrine. There is also a constant stream of visitors. Many poor pilgrims simply camp out in the tombs within the shrine enclosure, or by the side of the road, just outside the basti.

THE WALK

The lane that runs to the south of the Nizamuddin police station, (located on the roundabout just outside Humayun's tomb) takes you into the Nizamuddin basti. Turn right at the end of the lane and you will see signs that you are nearing the shrine—a narrow lane lined with shops selling flowers and other items for offering at the shrine. Follow this lane and after a few turns it will bring you to a gate leading into an enclosure. You can leave your footwear here and enter. There is an 'official' shoe deposit place where you might leave a few rupees as a tip, though it is not strictly required. Alternately if you buy flowers, the vendor will also look after your shoes for free.

Immediately as you enter you will see an enclosure made of stone screens that is painted green and white. This is the **tomb of Amir Khusro (1)**. He was born in 1253 in Etah in modern Uttar Pradesh and was a powerful courtier under several reigning emperors within his lifetime. He was also a devoted disciple and close friend of Nizamuddin Auliya. Amir Khusro was also a multifaceted genius, who is credited with a major role in the development of the Hindustani music tradition. He is even better known as a poet in Persian and Hindi, his eloquence earning him the sobriquet 'parrot of India'.

Though an influential nobleman, Amir Khusro spent a lot of time in the company of Nizamuddin and when the latter died he was heartbroken. He sat mourning beside the saint's grave until, six months later, he too was dead. The tomb building is of marble and is covered with a vaulted roof. It dates from 1605, built by a devotee, probably to replace a simpler structure. Only men may enter the inner grave enclosure.

South of the tomb of Amir Khusro is a 'dalan'—a pillared verandah, now covered with colour wash. This is the **dalan of Mirdha Ikram (2)**. Ikram, who died in 1801–02, was a mirdha or non-commissioned army officer under the Mughal emperor Shah Alam. He was buried here, as were some other members of his family.

It is customary to proceed to the **tomb of Nizamuddin Auliya (3)** after one has paid one's respects to his disciple Khusro. Nizamuddin's tomb is a marble building, very elaborately gilded and painted. Initially, Nizamuddin's grave was a very plain one, but over the centuries many elaborate structures were built over it, and most of the marble

structure seen today dates from the first quarter of the nineteenth century. The inner chamber is surrounded by a pillared verandah and topped by a bulbous, striped dome with a gilt finial on top. A distinctive feature is the elaborate parapet around the roof, which is made up of a mini arcade, topped by many small domes, each with a tiny pinnacle. At the four corners are chhatris, and below all this runs a deep chhajja.

It is immediately clear that there is a constant stream of devotees at the shrine of Nizamuddin. This swells into a packed crowd on Thursdays and during the Urs celebrations. Many who come are troubled by personal problems, medical conditions or financial difficulties. They ask the saint to intercede with God on their behalf. Others come back in gratitude when their prayers have been answered. Many come simply because it is a holy place and has a special atmosphere. Those who can afford to, often dispense charity at the dargah. This may take the form of donations with the khadims and pirzadas, who are the functionaries at the shrine. Or it may involve feeding the poor at one of the many eating places just outside the dargah. This keeps alive a tradition of charity that dates from the time of Nizamuddin.

The power of the prayers of Nizamuddin is legendary. Many prodigious feats have been attributed to him over the centuries. In 1303, when the emperor Alauddin Khalji was on the throne, the Mongols attacked and laid siege to Delhi (which at the time was centred at Mehrauli). After two months, they inexplicably retreated. Ziauddin Barani, the historian in whose lifetime (1285–1357) these events took place, attributed the mysterious withdrawal of the Mongols to the effect of the prayers of Nizamuddin.

To the west of the tomb of Nizamuddin is the **Jamat Khana mosque (4)**, the oldest building in the complex. Believed to have been built in the early fourteenth century by Khizr

It is best to orient yourself through the mosque which faces west. This will make it easier to navigate through the enclosure with the help of the following description.

Khan, the son of the emperor Alauddin Khalji, it has distinct similarities to the Alai Darwaza in the Qutub Minar complex. Look carefully for instance at the lotus bud fringe around the inside of the arches, for the combination of red sandstone and white marble (disguised beneath silver and red paint respectively) and the flattish domes. An interesting feature of the mosque is the spikes or spearheaded shapes that edge the roof. It is more usual for Sultanate period buildings to have a parapet of kanguras or merlons.

One story associated with the mosque is that its central chamber was originally built as a tomb for Nizamuddin Auliya during his lifetime. The saint however said that he did not wish to be buried there. Later therefore, a side chamber was added on either side of the central chamber, and it was converted into a mosque. On the other hand, architects have pointed out that the side chambers do not appear to be later additions.

There are several grave enclosures within the dargah complex. To the south-west of Nizamuddin's shrine is the **tomb of Jahanara (5)**. Jahanara was the daughter of the Mughal emperor Shahjahan, who accompanied him to Agra, when he was deposed by his son Aurangzeb and exiled to Agra. She died in 1681 and was buried in this

tomb that she had had commissioned during her own lifetime. The enclosure is made up of delicately carved, marble screens. Inside, there is more than one grave. The central one belongs to the princess. At its head is a slab of marble which has an inscription. Essentially this inscription tells us that this is the grave of Jahanara who was a devotee of the Chishti saints (the order to which Nizamuddin belonged), and that she wished that her grave be covered only by grass. Her wish was honoured to the extent that the marble gravestone has an open space in the middle. While grass originally grew in it, today it is mostly covered with rose petals strewn

by visitors. There are other graves too in Jahanara's enclosure. These belong to members of the Mughal royal family, from a later date.

Just east of Jahanara's tomb is the **tomb of Mohammad Shah (6)**. He was the Mughal emperor who reigned from 1719–48 and was nicknamed Rangila or literally 'colourful' for his pleasure-loving lifestyle and his special interest in poetry and music. The Mughal Empire was already in decline when he ascended the throne, but he was the last Mughal emperor to rule with a semblance of power. One catastrophic event of his reign was the invasion of the Persian emperor Nadir Shah in 1739. On his return from Delhi, Nadir Shah took away vast treasure, including the famed Peacock

Throne of the Mughal emperors.

The tomb of Mohammad Shah stands exactly between Nizamuddin's and Amir Khusro's, and it is said that his coming between the two friends brought a curse upon the Mughal royal family, which never flourished after that. The tomb enclosure truly represents the artistic refinement of the age, as it is exquisitely and elaborately carved from white marble. Even the leaves of the door are of marble, beautifully carved with a floral pattern.

There are several graves inside the enclosure. The largest one is that of the emperor. To the west of him lies his wife, Nawab Sahiba Mahal. At the foot of her grave is that of her daughter who was given in marriage to the son of Nadir Shah. Next to her grave is that of her baby, as in all likelihood she died in childbirth. The other graves are of lesser-known members of the royal family.

To the east of Mohammad Shah's tomb is the grave enclosure of **Mirza Jahangir (7),** who represents the last phase of the Mughal dynasty. His father, Akbar II, who was on the throne from 1806 to 1837, was a pensioner of the British East India Company and an emperor in less than name. His territories were actually administered by the British. Akbar II wanted his younger son Jahangir, to succeed him on the throne, but the British insisted that his firstborn Zafar was entitled to succeed. Jahangir, who was an impetuous young man, took up a confrontationist stance. At the Red Fort, one of the prince's followers fired on the party of the British Resident who was the highest administrative official stationed in Delhi. Though no one was hurt, Jahangir was arrested and later exiled to Allahabad. He ultimately died there and his body was brought back to Delhi for burial.

This tomb enclosure, like the previous two, is made of elaborately carved marble screens. The grave of Jahangir is the second from the west. The gravestone is beautifully carved with a pattern of leaves and flowers. Curiously its design is that of a woman's grave, as it has the typically flat, rectangular takhti or slate on it. Clearly then, it belonged to a woman's grave and for reasons unknown, was removed from there to be placed over Jahangir's body. To the west of Jahangir's grave is that of his brother Babur. In this case too, the stone originally belonged to another grave and bears an inscription which dates from 1579–80. Two other graves in the enclosure belong to unknown persons, most certainly from the Mughal royal family.

8

One doorway leads out of this enclosure to the east, into a space known as the **house of Mirza Jahangir (8)**. The name should not be understood to mean that this is where Mirza Jahangir lived. This is simply where members of the family were buried, (for a similar use see 'dalan of Mirdha Ikram' above). Though most of the graves here are unmarked, one has an inscription that tells us that it is the grave of the wife of Mirza Babur.

9

Go back into the main shrine courtyard and go out through the gateway to the north of Nizamuddin's tomb. A few twists in the narrow passageway will bring you to the **baoli of Nizamuddin (9),** that is a large, open source of ground-water. A wide flight of steps leads down to the water on the northern side. A number of tombs have been built around the baoli, particularly along the western side; but while one has glimpses of interesting architecture from the baoli, they are otherwise inaccessible to the public. The baoli dates to the lifetime of the saint and has some interesting stories attached to it.

It is said that at the same time as Nizamuddin was having it built in 1321, the emperor Ghiyasuddin Tughlaq began work on the mammoth fortifications at Tughlaqabad (now in south Delhi). The emperor decreed that all workmen would spend the entire working day at his project, but the workmen continued to work on the baoli at night. The enraged ruler prohibited the sale of oil, so that they would have no lamps to light their work, but through the miraculous powers of the saint, the water of the baoli effectively worked as oil for the lamps. The baoli was completed,

Nizamuddin blessed its water, and ever since it has been believed to work wonderful cures.

From the baoli go back to the shrine courtyard and out through the gateway through which you first entered. Collect your shoes, then follow the path back just a bit until you climb up a few steps and come to a fork in the path. Turn left, and then right, which will shortly bring you into **Atgah Khan's tomb (10)**.

Atgah Khan, whose given name was Shamsuddin Mohammad, was an important nobleman at the court of the emperor Humayun, to whom he displayed a high degree of loyalty when the emperor was defeated by Sher Shah. His wife, Jiji, was given the honour of being the wet nurse of Humayun's son Akbar, with the customary title 'Angah'. Her husband thus got the title 'Atgah' along with his other titles from the court. As Akbar ascended the throne in 1556 at the tender age of thirteen, his wet nurses and their families remained influential at his court for a long time. In particular, the family of another wet nurse, Maham Angah, was engaged in a rivalry with Jiji Angah's family. Maham Angah's son, Adham Khan, murdered Shamsuddin Mohammad, for which Akbar punished him by having him thrown from the ramparts of the fort at Agra, where this incident took place in 1562. The body of Shamsuddin Khan was brought to Delhi and buried here. The building was constructed over the remains in 1566–67 by Atgah Khan's son, Mirza Aziz Kokaltash. Kokaltash literally means 'foster brother' in Turkish, which was the mother tongue of the Mughals. It was a title received by Mirza Aziz as he was the son of Akbar's wet nurse, Jiji Angah.

The tomb of Atgah Khan is a beautiful example of the architecture of Akbar's reign. The most striking ornamentation on the outside are the beautiful geometric patterns made up of an inlay of mainly red and yellow sandstone and white and black marble and coloured tiles. Besides this there is low relief carving, stone screens, and wide bands of calligraphy with verses from the Quran carved in stone. Inside, there are remains of some finely incised and painted plaster. There are three graves inside. The central one is that of Atgah Khan, the one to its east is that of Jiji Angah and the other is unidentified.

To the west of the tomb is a wall mosque, decorated with beautiful coloured tiles that are unfortunately, very damaged. The bright blue, green and yellow pigments, derived from crushed, coloured stones, have not faded through the centuries. In the south-western corner is a dalan or pillared hall, which was used as a khanqah for Sufis. The slender pillars and cusped arches of this structure suggest that it dates from the late Mughal period, maybe the eighteenth century.

11

Once you leave Atgah Khan's tomb trace your way back through the path leading to the dargah, past the shops until you come out into the open. Keep going straight, and you will soon find a Mughal era sandstone gateway to your right. Enter it, and to your right again you will find a doorway leading into an enclosure. This contains the building known as **Chaunsath Khamba (11)**, literally 'sixty-four pillars', which is the tomb of Mirza Aziz Kokaltash.

Built during Mirza Aziz's lifetime, the tomb is a large, open pavilion made of marble. It actually has sixty-four pillars, as you will find if you count carefully. There are groups of four closely set pillars at each of the four corners, totalling sixteen. Between the corners, along the four sides there are four double pillars that add up to thirty-two. Within the hall there are sixteen single pillars, making it sixty-four in all.

The ornamentation of the hall is minimal, both inside and out. There is very little carving and it is the overall form and the large expanses of marble that are the principal attractive features. Some time far in the past, (certainly before the late nineteenth century) missing portions of the screen were rebuilt in pale-coloured sandstone, which is fairly obvious. The graves inside the pavilion are made of beautifully carved marble. The large one, second from the west, is that of Mirza Aziz, and the one to its west, is that of his wife. The other graves are presumed to be of other members of the family. There are many other graves in the yard immediately outside the tomb, some of them quite beautifully carved out of sandstone. Some of these are said to belong to the daughters of Bahadur Shah, the last Mughal emperor.

A doorway in the northern wall of the enclosure in which Chaunsath Khamba stands, leads into another enclosure. This contains the **tomb of Mirza Asadullah Khan Ghalib**

(12) who lived from 1797–1869 and is the famous poet of Urdu and Persian. He lived at a time when the Mughal emperor simply existed as a pensioner of the British East India Company's government, and therefore could not afford to patronize poets, painters, musicians and builders on the lavish scale customary for his

ancestors. The new government had different priorities, and represented a different way of life with different tastes. Ghalib therefore spent most of his life in some financial difficulty, to which were added the tribulations of the uprising of 1857 which was suppressed very harshly by the British. He died in 1869 and was buried in a very simple grave. Later, in the middle of the twentieth century, a tomb was commissioned by the Ghalib Memorial Society and designed by the Hyderabad architect, Zain Yar Jang. It is a fairly plain but fitting structure.

Return to the Mathura Road the way you came, and if you are feeling adventurous, cross this very busy road to look at the **Sabz Burj (13)** situated on the roundabout in the middle of the road. Believed to date from the early Mughal period (1530s or 1540s), this is the tomb of a now unknown person, and its name literally means 'green tower'. With its slightly bulbous dome placed on a very high cylindrical drum, it does somewhat resemble a tower. This was probably more so when it had all its original tiles and as the name suggests, it might have been predominantly green. The tiles on the dome were replaced in the 1980s. The distinctive features of this building are Timurid in style, characteristic of the architecture created by Timur or Tamerlane and his immediate descendants in Samarkand and Herat. The Mughals were descendants of Timur and their architecture in India too owes much to this legacy. Similarities with buildings of Central Asia, as in Samarkand, are quite apparent, including the tall drum and high pesh taqs (projecting façades) on the four long sides.

Of the ornamentation that remains today, the painted plaster in the arched niches on the outside is noteworthy. For many years during British rule, Sabz Burj, was used as a police station. Sometime in the 1920s, the police station was moved out to its present location, beside the road.

13

HUMAYUN'S TOMB
COMPLEX

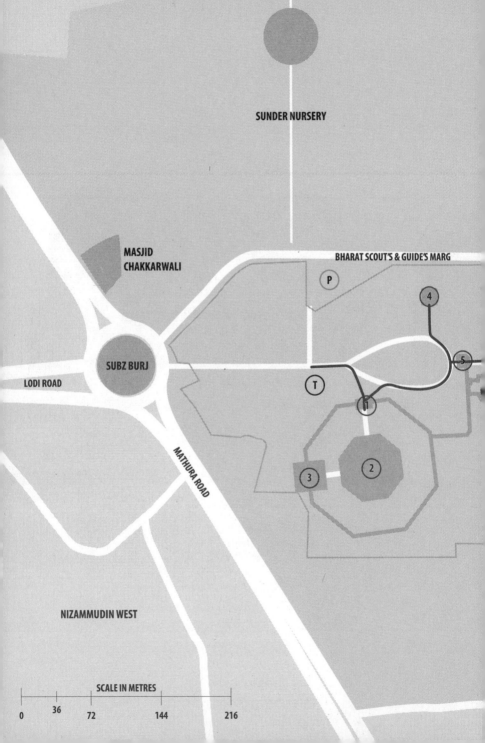

SUNDER NURSERY

MASJID CHAKKARWALI

BHARAT SCOUT'S & GUIDE'S MARG

P

SUBZ BURJ

LODI ROAD

T

MATHURA ROAD

4

5

1

2

3

NIZAMMUDIN WEST

SCALE IN METRES

0   36   72   144   216

HUMAYUN'S TOMB

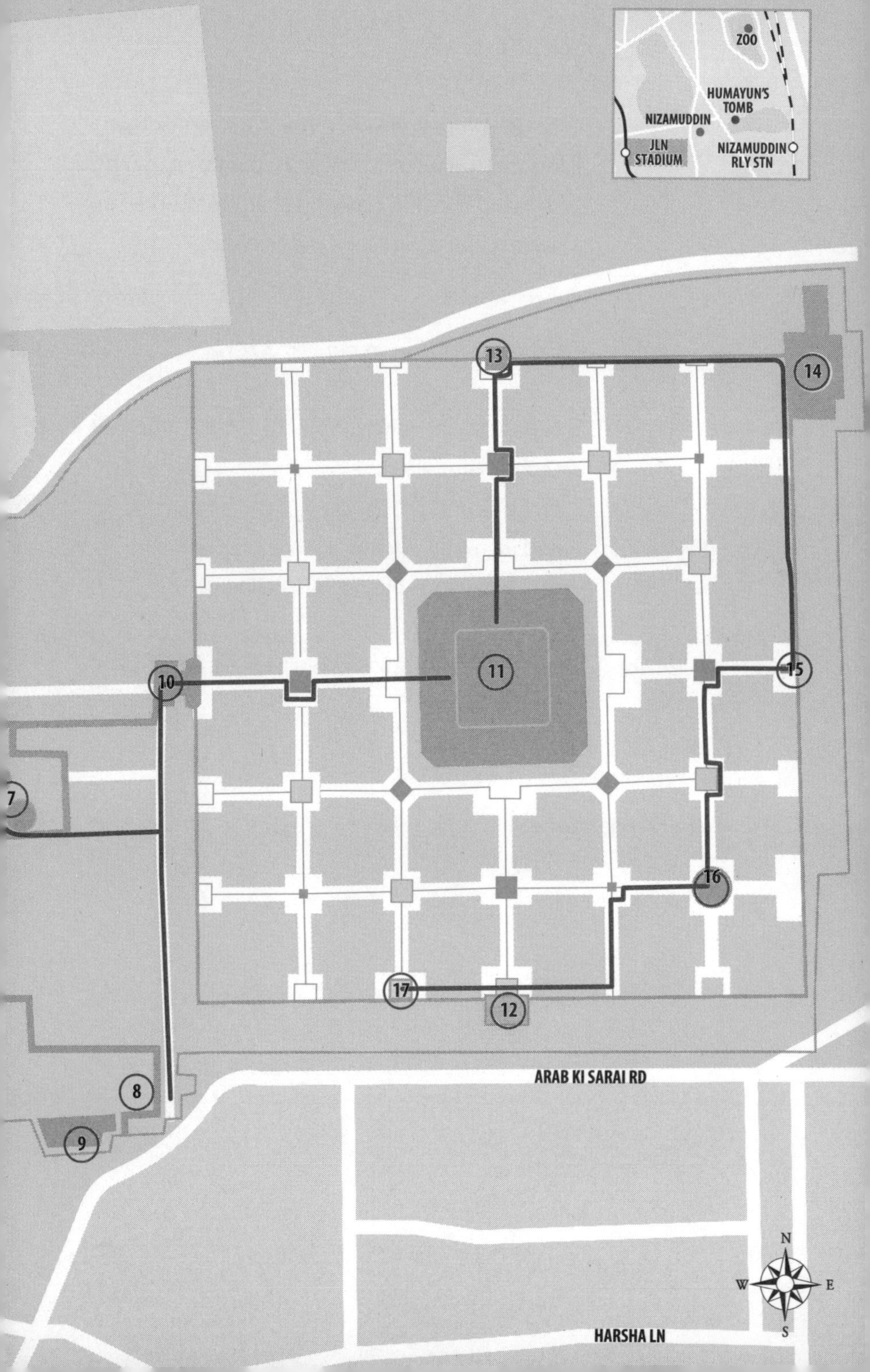

ZOO

HUMAYUN'S TOMB

NIZAMUDDIN

JLN STADIUM

NIZAMUDDIN RLY STN

13

14

11

10

7

15

16

17

12

ARAB KI SARAI RD

8

9

N
W   E
S

HARSHA LN

Timings: Sunrise to sunset.

Tickets: Citizens of India and SAARC countries (Afghanistan, Bangladesh, Bhutan, Maldives, Nepal, Pakistan and Sri Lanka) and BIMSTEC countries (Bangladesh, Bhutan, Myanmar, Nepal, Sri Lanka and Thailand) .... ₹10

Others: .... US$5 / ₹250

Children up to 15 years old .... free

Highlights: Isa Khan's tomb, Humayun's tomb, barber's tomb (best for an abbreviated walk).

Difficulty Level: Paved pathways through the complex. Some ramps for wheelchair access but not into buildings.

Metro Station: Jawaharlal Nehru Stadium on the Violet line, 1.5 kms.

Amenities: Washrooms.

Parking: On site.

MUGHAL MAUSOLEUM

Humayun died in January 1556, at the age of fifty-one. He had constructed in Delhi a fortress known as Dinpanah (now called Purana Qila), beside the river Yamuna. Upon his death, he left behind an empire that was precariously held together. It had only been a few months since he had regained control of the territories of India, after fifteen years of exile, following his defeat at the hands of Sher Shah Sur in 1540. His son Akbar, who inherited the throne, was only thirteen years old and was, or rather his generals were, immediately faced with the task of dealing with insurrections in many parts of the empire.

The first four or five years of Akbar's reign saw the consolidation of the empire, mainly through the efforts of Bairam Khan, Akbar's tutor and regent. Bairam Khan's power and some of his policies had made him unpopular with other influential people at court, including the family of Akbar's wet nurse, Maham Angah. Akbar was soon persuaded to shake himself free of the influence of Bairam Khan who departed for Mecca, but on the way he was killed. Maham Angah's power did not last long either and she died soon after.

So by 1562 Akbar had come of age, and this was when he started work on the mausoleum of his father. Humayun's chief wife, Haji Begam, is often credited with the building of his tomb but in fact, she was away most of the time on pilgrimage, and Akbar merely put her in charge during some of the time that she was in Delhi. The scale of the project and its timing clearly suggests that the young emperor himself was responsible for commissioning it.

The site chosen for the mausoleum was significant. It was just a kilometre and a half south of the fortress built by Humayun. It was picturesquely situated beside the river, though since then the river has moved considerably eastwards. It was also fairly close to the holy shrine of the Sufi saint, Nizamuddin Auliya. The saint's shrine had prompted the practice of many burials in the vicinity, and Humayun's tomb was simply the most monumental among these. Finally, it was located on the road to Agra, where Akbar's capital had shifted in 1558.

THE WALK

The area contains many buildings apart from Humayun's tomb and this walk will take in those that are within the ticketed walled area. The entrance opens into a green area and the path curving to your right will bring you to the **tomb of Isa Khan Niyazi (1-3)**. He was an Afghan who was one of the most important nobles of Sher Shah Sur and his successor Islam Shah Sur. He built this tomb within his own lifetime, in 1547–48, and clearly intended it to be a sort of family mausoleum as there are a number of graves within it, all uninscribed.

Enter the enclosure through the ruined **gateway (1)**; notice how the carved corbels of grey quartzite frame the top of the doorway. This is a hangover from the typical architecture of the pre-Delhi Sultanate period, when Indian builders spanned space using techniques based on horizontal beams placed on vertical columns. The Sultanate architects introduced the use of the arch to India, but also adopted indigenous Indian forms which they used from time to time, such as in this doorway. The structure around the doorway is in ruins, so you can see the materials out of which the core was constructed. These basically consist of rough stones held together by a mortar that contained limestone, brick powder, and a variety of organic material including cow dung, jaggery, lentils, greens, and the viscous pulp of bael or wood apple. These materials produced a mortar that was durable, but could also breathe. A side effect is that organic growth tends to take place on these buildings, giving them a dark patina, which is harmless, though some might consider it unsightly.

2

The gateway leads to an octagonal garden within an enclosing wall. In the centre is an octagonal **tomb (2)**. It has some characteristic features of late Sultanate octagonal tombs. The verandah is made of double pillars, and the corners have sloping buttresses. Above the verandah is a sloping chhajja, and the roof has an edge made by a pattern of kanguras, which in a fortification are a part of the defensive battlements but here, are simply a decorative motif. Eight chhatris or pillared kiosks on the roof surround the central dome that has a lotus-shaped crest on top.

The stone used in the lower part of the building is quartzite, which is widely available in Delhi, with some details picked

out in red sandstone. The upper parts of the structure are covered in limestone plaster. The embellishments are also typical of the late Sultanate period— finely incised plaster and tile work, mostly in brilliant blue and green mineral pigments. Walk around to the back, to the southern side, facing away from the entrance gateway. This is the entrance into the tomb and the façade is decorated slightly more elaborately. Conventionally, in all Islamic burials, the body is placed such that the head is to the north and the feet to the south, and the face is turned towards Mecca, which in India is to the west. Most tomb buildings are entered from the south.

Inside the tomb, there are several cenotaphs, which mark the position of the burial, since the actual burial is deep within the ground. Isa Khan's grave, though uninscribed, is probably the one in the middle, on the northern side. Let your eyes adjust to the darkness inside and then look at the ceiling, which is beautifully decorated with incised and painted stucco or plaster.

To the west of the tomb is a **mosque (3),** which was probably built at the same time. Here too notice the beautiful tile work in bright blue, green and yellow. Inside, the west wall is marked out by three red sandstone mihrabs. This enclosure containing the tomb and grave came to be used as homes sometime in the eighteenth century by a large population from whom it was acquired in the early twentieth century by the Archaeological Survey of India, and conserved.

It is easier to orient yourself if you remember that the entrance from beside the ticket window, where you first entered, is at the extreme west of the complex.

3

Leave the enclosure and get back into the open green space you first entered. At the far end you will see a square platform, which is the **tomb of Bu Halima (4)**. At ground level is the burial chamber in the centre, and it is surrounded by smaller chambers. It is not known who Bu Halima was, but the architectural features of this tomb suggest that it was probably built in the late sixteenth century. The tomb was originally set in a walled garden and a part of the enclosing wall can be seen surrounding the tomb platform on the north, east and west. The corners are topped by chhatris decorated with tiles. The enclosure was originally rectangular, but the west wall was removed in the early twentieth century to make this the main entrance to Humayun's tomb. Bu Halima's garden too was occupied by a resident population until its acquisition in the early twentieth century.

At the eastern end of this garden, directly opposite the ticket window entrance is a plain looking **gateway (5)** finished in white plaster that leads to Bu Halima's garden. Walk through it and you will come out towards what was clearly its 'right' side. It is nicely proportioned and shaped. Note the two beautiful tile work medallions in the spandrels of the large arch.

To the south-west of this gate, and set at right angles to it, is the **gate of Arab Sarai (6)**. It is said that when Haji Begam, Humayun's widow, came back from her pilgrimage to Mecca, she brought with her 300 Arabs and built this complex to house them. The gate is an attractive example of early Mughal architecture. At this time there was a shift away from the limestone plaster decoration that was popular under the Lodi dynasty, to the use of inlay patterns in different coloured stones. This gateway has a background of neatly cut golden-grey quartzite, with

decorative details in red sandstone inlaid with white marble. Look at the intricate rosettes set in the spandrels on either side of the arches, and the fairly simple but beautiful border running across the top. Also notice the jharokhas supported on elaborately carved brackets.

Enter through the gateway and you will notice that not much is left inside. This was in fact a well populated neighbourhood until the early twentieth century, and in typical Delhi terms it was a comparatively 'good address', in contrast for instance to the settlement in Isa Khan's tomb. Conservation work by the Archaeological Survey removed the houses within, leaving the older and bigger structures. A little way in, to your left, are two buildings next to each other—the **Afsarwala tomb and mosque (7)**—the name simply means the 'officer's tomb and mosque' and nothing further is known of the patron, or who is buried here.

These buildings too show some typically early Mughal features. The tomb is essentially square, but chamfered or with the corners cut off, which gives it the shape of an irregular octagon. The dome is placed on a high drum and it is actually a 'double dome'. This means that there is an outer dome in proportion with the outer dimensions of the building; and within it is a smaller dome which is better suited to the proportions of the inner chamber. The Mughals popularized the double dome in India. One of the graves inside has the date 1566–67 on it, so this tomb is at least as old as that.

The mosque next to the tomb was most likely built at the same time. It looks quite plain and rough, because the red plaster that covered it has mostly fallen off. Inside, built against the qibla wall, is a minbar from which the imam or

priest led the prayers. On the other side of the mosque is a low chamber which is believed to have been a hammam.

Taking the path that leads south-east of these buildings you enter another enclosure which is the **Jahangiri mandi (8)**. It is said that this was a wholesale market (mandi) built during the reign of the emperor Jahangir (1605–27) by the chief eunuch, Mihrban Agha. Known as khwajasara, some eunuchs were put in charge of the royal harems and thus became powerful and influential. Walk out through the gate which is at the eastern end of the enclosure to see its façade of cream plaster and tile panels. The inscription in red sandstone on either side at the top of the arch tells us that it was built by Mihrban Agha in the reign of Jahangir.

Inside, the ruined rooms along the long edges of the rectangular enclosure must have been shops, with probably store rooms behind them. At the western end of the enclosure is another gate, quite plain, which led to another part of Arab Sarai. Against the southern wall is a **baoli (9)**. Examine it carefully. You don't want to fall in! In style, it is not like other baolis in Delhi, which usually have a single broad flight of stairs leading down to the water. It is said that it is modelled on baolis found in the Malwa region of central India.

Go back the way you came, on the path that you took from Afsarwala tomb. Continue straight on that path and it will bring you out right beside the **western gate to Humayun's tomb (10)**. Note the six-pointed star on either side of the arched entrance. This kind of star is a cosmic symbol common to several religions including Hinduism and Islam.

Also note the chhatris at the corners on top of the gate. The western gate was not originally the main entrance to the tomb. As you notice there were many enclosures between it and the main road. Now it is where all visitors enter the inner complex.

As you pass through the gate you get your first glimpse of the magnificent **Humayun's Tomb (11)**. Set in a large square garden, this was probably the first char-bagh tomb in India, or a tomb set in a garden, divided on a grid pattern by walkways and water channels. The garden today, though beautiful, does not look exactly as it did when the tomb was built. In the climate of north India expanses of grass were not practical— they soaked up water and provided no shade. The gardens under the Mughals would have consisted of flowering and fruit trees and bushes. By the second half of the nineteenth century the garden of the tomb had

11

been destroyed by neglect, and later restorations paid little attention to the original layout of paths and water channels. The new landscaping of the early twentieth century was responsible for the extensive lawns, which were a part of the British colonial idea of the ideal garden. In the early years of this century a revitalization project was carried out in the gardens which restored the old pattern of water channels and paths. At this time some low trees were also planted, keeping in mind the varieties that would have been popular in Mughal times. You can see these in clumps, mainly at the edges of the lawns.

Stop and take in the large and spectacular tomb from afar. The top of the finial of the dome is some fifty metres above the level of the ground. For comparison, this makes it more than two-thirds the height of the Qutub Minar. Look at some of the distinctive features of the building. It was designed and executed by the architect Mirak Mirza Ghiyas, who was of Iranian descent and had worked in Central Asia as well as India. The building thus combines principles from different building traditions.

In shape the dome is very typical of Central and West Asian buildings of the time. It bulges slightly above the drum, and is pulled up to a point at the top. Unlike most such domes

there is no lotus crest on top, and the finial rises directly from the dome. This finial, which is in the form of a number of copper vessels on top of each other, is itself nearly six metres tall. However unlike the tile work that was popular in these Central and West Asia, this dome is covered in marble, and in fact the use of stone for decoration was a very Indian tradition. The surface of the building is decorated in a very striking way. Bold inlay patterns outline the shapes and planes of the structural form—such as arches and rectangular panels. The stone used is red and yellow sandstone, and black and white marble. Chhatris of various sizes and at various levels around the dome provide an interesting outline at the roof level— again a very Indian feature.

Come closer to the building and look at the red sandstone covered platform on which it sits. There are arched recesses that run in a row right around the platform. The entrances set into them lead into a total of 124 chambers. In one of them is the grave of Humayun and the others house the many graves of family members who were buried there over the course of several centuries. Do not climb the platform just yet, turn right and walk along its edge and turn left so you are alongside the southern edge of the platform. When you get to the middle of this side of the platform, climb up the stairs to the top. The tomb is designed to be approached from the south, and if you look across the garden you will see the **southern entrance gateway (12)**. It is wider and more elaborate than the western one. Its full size and splendour can best be appreciated from outside the complex, so if you have the time after the walk, you might like to go to the residential area known as Nizamuddin East. Here, from the road that runs around the northern periphery of the houses, you can get a good view of this gate.

For now, you can concentrate your attention on the tomb. The ornamentation mostly consists of large panels of inlaid stone. There is a relatively small amount of stone carving. For instance look at the slender pillars (called engaged pilasters) that are attached to the corners of the entrance arches. Towards the bottom, the red sandstone has been finely carved in a herringbone pattern, with the rounded shape of a kalash below it. The kalash-shape carving was frequently used in Islamic tombs and even mosques in India, and is clear evidence of the cultural synthesis that developed in the medieval period.

As you step into the entrance chamber, the ceiling is worth looking at as it has some intricately carved and painted limestone plaster. Step through into the central tomb chamber. Its large size is emphasized by its emptiness and plainness, but it was not always thus. Seventeenth century British traveller, William Finch, described the floor as being covered in rich carpets, the cenotaph covered in a white sheet with a canopy overhead, and also little tables holding the emperor's Quran, his shoes, turban and sword. The Venetian traveller, Nicolao Manucci, described the walls and ceiling as

'It is adorned inside with many paintings and stones of various kinds, and the roof of the dome is gilded... over the tomb a coverlet made of rich brocade. At the sides of this covering are placed the arms of the dead king... his quiver full of arrows, his bow, his sword, his dagger or poignard, lance, musket...' (Niccolao Manucci, *Storia do Mogor*, 1653–1708)

being decorated with paintings, stones and gilt. So what has happened to the tomb since?

'It was from these vaults, after Delhi had fallen, in September 1857, that "Hodson, of Hodson's Horse" ... dragged out the last of the Moghuls, the puppet king who had been the nominal head of the rebellion. The coffin of his ancestor could not shield the trembling old intriguer.'
(Sidney Low, *A Vision of India*, 1906)

The mausoleum was maintained by successive emperors of the dynasty and many members of the royal family were buried in the crypt below (where there are more than 150 graves). In 1857 the uprising against British rule took place and Delhi was a major centre. Bahadur Shah, pen named 'Zafar', was at the time on the throne, as a pensioner of the British with no real sovereign powers of his own, and he became a leader of the uprising. When the British re-conquered Delhi, Bahadur Shah and members of his family escaped to Humayun's tomb and took shelter in it. The British finally came to arrest them from here, and presumably it was at that time that the tomb was despoiled. Nothing more was heard of its contents.

Despite being bare the chamber is atmospheric. Notice how the stone jalis that fill the windows let in a filtered light. The patterns of the jalis vary, generally becoming finer in the smaller windows. The western side, which is the qibla has an arch-shaped panel set in the screen. The dome rises beautifully in an uninterrupted manner from the sides. The net pattern, which forms the curve between the arches, was typical of Mughal architecture. The dome is a double dome.

Leave the central chamber and you can visit some of the side chambers in the building. There are a number of marble cenotaphs in them. Most are unmarked but Humayun's wives, Hamida Banu begam and Biga begam, are believed to be buried in the chamber in the north-east corner, and his daughters in the south-east corner chamber. If you come out and walk around on the large platform on which the tomb is built you will see more cenotaphs. Most do not have the names of those who are buried here, but local tradition ascribes identities to them. For instance the cenotaph closest to the steps on the north side is that of Dara Shikoh, the scholarly and mystically inclined eldest son of Shahjahan, who was put to death by his brother Aurangzeb who then usurped the throne.

Leave the platform on the northern side and walk down the path to the building set against the wall at the extreme end. This is the **northern pavilion (13)** with a small pool that might have been used as a bath. Outside the boundary wall at this point is a well, the water of which is used to feed the channels in the garden. It flows through the building and down a chute.

Walking along the wall, in an easterly direction from this building will bring you to another building set in the corner of the garden. This is the **north-eastern pavilion (14)**, which would have overlooked the river. Notice the open plan and the beautiful, red sandstone pillars. Continue walking along this eastern wall of the garden. See how the ground level falls away from the level at the tomb platform. This was the natural slope of the land towards the river, which was landscaped into a terrace. In the middle of the wall there is the quite elaborate **eastern pavilion (15)**, with a pillared verandah and arcaded rooms.

Getting off this pavilion you will see a building in the south-

eastern part of the garden. This is known as the **barber's tomb (16)**, though it is not known who exactly is buried here. The popular name by which it is known is most likely not related to any historical fact. If there ever was a barber influential enough to justify a grand tomb within the tomb garden of the emperor himself, he probably would have found mention in the historical record. The tomb building is interesting—note the elaborate dome drum, which brings to mind, in a highly stylized manner of course, a battlemented fort wall. It has a border of kanguras punctuated by little turrets. Of the two cenotaphs inside, the one with the takhti has a date inscribed on it which corresponds to 1590. The other grave is that of a man, which is apparent from the qalamdan on it.

In the middle of the wall on the southern side of the garden enclosure is the **southern gate (12)** of Humayun's tomb, mentioned before. It has a number of rooms, and for quite a while under British rule it was used as a rest house for visitors. A little to its west is a small **mosque (17)** built, sometime in the eighteenth century, of blue-grey quartzite stone.

RED FORT

MAHATMA GANDHI MARG

(13)
(12)
(10)
(9)
(8)

(14)
(11)

(15)
(17)
(16)

(3)
(3)
(3)
(3)

(3)

SHYAMA PRASAD MUKHERJI MARG

(T)

ANGURI
BAGH
MKT

SCALE IN METRES

0   40   80   160   240

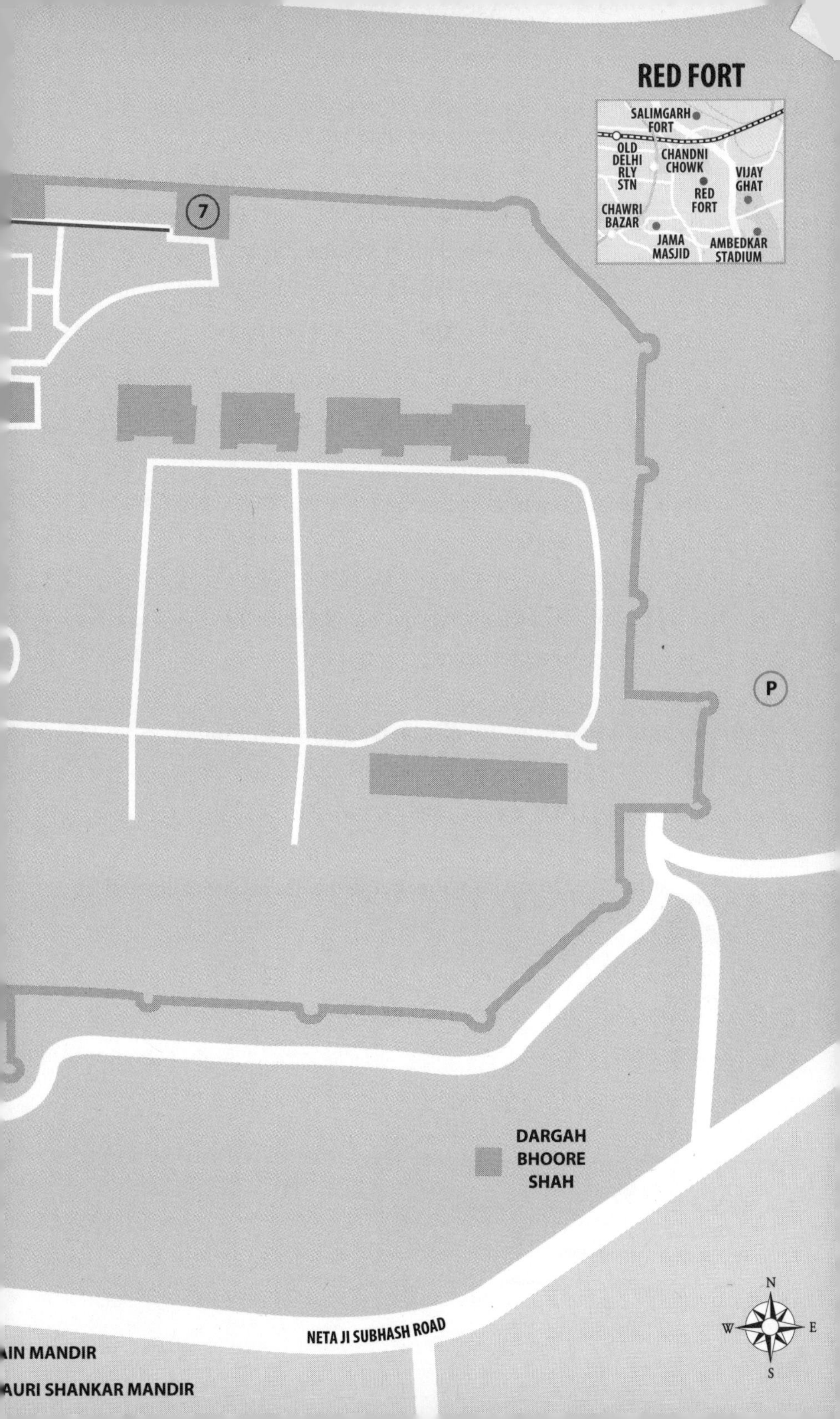

RED FORT

SALIMGARH FORT

OLD DELHI RLY STN

CHANDNI CHOWK

CHAWRI BAZAR

RED FORT

VIJAY GHAT

JAMA MASJID

AMBEDKAR STADIUM

7

P

DARGAH
BHOORE
SHAH

NETA JI SUBHASH ROAD

AIN MANDIR

AURI SHANKAR MANDIR

N
W   E
S

Timings:	Sunrise to sunset; closed on Mondays.
Tickets:	Citizens of India and SAARC countries (Afghanistan, Bangladesh, Bhutan, Maldives, Nepal, Pakistan and Sri Lanka) and BIMSTEC countries (Bangladesh, Bhutan, Myanmar, Nepal, Sri Lanka and Thailand) ₹10
	Others: US$5 / ₹250
	Children up to 15 years old free
Highlights:	Diwan-e-Aam, Diwan-e-Khas, Khas Mahal, Hayat Baksh Bagh.
Difficulty Level:	Paved pathways through the complex. Wheelchair access to most buildings.
Metro Station:	Chandni Chowk on the Yellow line, 1 km.
Amenities:	Washrooms, café.
Parking:	On site (near the southern or Delhi Gate of the fort).

ROYAL CITADEL

Red Fort is the popular colloquial name for this magnificent palace complex. Its name during Mughal times was Qila-e-Mubarak ('auspicious citadel') or Qila-e-Shahjahanabad (the 'fort of the city of Shahjahanabad'). It was an important part of the new capital city, Shahjahanabad that the Mughal emperor Shahjahan established in the middle of the seventeenth century.

It is said that Shahjahan was fed up with Agra (also called Akbarabad), which had been the capital continuously from the time of his grandfather Akbar. It was hot, it was crowded, the fort was small, but probably most of all, it did not afford full scope for Shahjahan to indulge his passion for building. By the late 1630s one major project in Agra,

the Taj Mahal, was well under way and Shahjahan needed something new to occupy his attention. Delhi had a long history as an imperial capital, under the Turks during the Delhi Sultanate, and in the early part of the Mughal dynasty, when his great-grandfather Humayun had established the city of Dinpanah. It is said that Shahjahan visited Delhi several times, and with the advice of the royal astrologers and doctors, settled on a site on the bank of the Yamuna for the new city and its citadel. It was located further north than all the previous cities of Delhi, just south of a small fort called Salimgarh that had been constructed in 1546 under orders of Salim Shah, the Sur ruler.

The foundation stone for the fort of Shahjahanabad was laid on 16 April 1639. Two master builders were appointed— Ustad Hamid and Ustad Ahmad; and the overall supervision of construction was entrusted to a series of officials, the last of them being Makramat Khan. Over a hundred lakhs of rupees (₹10,000,000) were spent, about half on the walls of the fort and half on the buildings within. Just over nine years later, Shahjahan entered the fort for its inauguration on 17 May 1648. The splendours of the darbar (ceremonial court) that was held on that and other subsequent occasions have been described by historians in detail.

The glory days of the fort did not last very long. In 1658 Shahjahan was deposed by his son Aurangzeb, and lived the rest of his life as a prisoner in Agra. Aurangzeb, busy with campaigns in his extensive and increasingly hard-to-manage empire, did not spend much time in Delhi. In temperament too he was, very unlike his father and most of his ancestors, not in favour of much opulence and ostentation. Over the years there were signs of increasing austerity in court ceremonials. Music in court was discontinued, and so was the practice of celebrating the emperor's birthday by weighing him against gold and silver and distributing the proceeds to charity. The fort must have been a fairly sombre place during his reign.

Aurangzeb's successors were not all like him. In fact Mohammad Shah 'Rangila', the 'colourful' (1718–48), was very fond of poetry, music and dance. However, after Aurangzeb's death in 1707, the Mughal Empire was very much in decline. Through the eighteenth century there were many changes in succession, with many of the emperors being mere puppets of more powerful ministers. Territories and resources too were shrinking. Regional powers were carving up parts of the erstwhile empire between them. To top it all there were at least two important occasions when the city or the fort was sacked. The first was in 1739, when the Persian ruler Nadir Shah invaded Mughal territories right up to Delhi and went back with a huge tribute. Then in 1788, the Afghan, Rohilla Ghulam Qadir sacked the fort and blinded the emperor Shah Alam II.

By then the British East India Company was the new power on the scene and began to rule Delhi in 1803. The Mughal emperor became a mere pensioner, living on a small allow-

ance within the fort with hundreds of near and distant relatives to support. Then in 1857 there was a widespread revolt against British rule, and the then emperor Bahadur Shah, and some of his close relatives took an active part in it. When Delhi was recaptured by the British, Bahadur Shah was exiled to Burma, all the occupants of the fort were turned out and it was occupied by the British army.

Today the fort is a tourist attraction and one of Delhi's three attractions inscribed by UNESCO on its list of World Heritage Sites.

THE WALK

The gate through which visitors now enter was not there when Shahjahan was emperor. In the original plan, the gateway to the fort directly faced the broad street running down the middle of the city of Shahjahanabad, now known as Chandni Chowk. Sometime during the early part of his reign, Aurangzeb (reigned 1658–1707) had a barbican or outer defence constructed in front of the actual gate, and that is what you today go through first. It is said that when he heard of this construction, Shahjahan wrote to Aurangzeb lamenting the fact that the latter had treated the fort like a bride, putting a veil before her face.

You go through the outer gate to enter a quadrangle formed by the barbican, and what you see to the left is the original gate to the fort, the **Lahore Gate (1)**—so named because it faces west and in the direction of Lahore, an important Mughal city. This certainly looks more impressive as a gate and has some interesting decorative features typical of the architecture of Shahjahan's reign. Look for instance at the row of small chhatris at the top, and the subtle low relief carving that decorates the surface of the stone. Just below the chhatris is a row of kanguras with a decorative edge. These are to be found all along the fort wall on the outside as well.

Look around you. The top of the barbican wall that encloses this gate is now shorn of its battlements, covered with earth and planted with grass. At one end encased in sandstone but nevertheless unmistakable, is an elevator shaft. This carries, among other important persons, the prime minister to the top from where he/she addresses the nation every year on 15 August, India's Independence Day.

Walk through the Lahore Gate and the long covered passage you enter is the **Chhatta Bazaar (2)**, literally 'shopping arcade'. The shops on either side which now sell articles to tourists once sold high quality goods to inhabitants of the fort and visitors. Notice how halfway down, the arcade opens up into a square open-to-the-sky. This was once a very beautiful place, with the plastered walls painted with verses from the Quran and floral patterns.

You emerge from the arcade into a large open space which is the interior of the fort. Here you must begin to exercise your imagination because the fort today looks nothing like it did in Shahjahan's time. As you move around the fort you essentially perceive it as a large open space dotted with buildings. This is not how a seventeenth century visitor or even one in the first half of the nineteenth century would have experienced it. Coming through the Chhatta Bazaar he would have instead found himself in a large courtyard, some 60 metres square, surrounded by colonnades. Here the emperor's guard was stationed, and here the visitor would have to dismount, leaving his horse or carriage in the court before proceeding further.

If that visitor had looked left or right, he would have seen an arcaded street leading in either direction from the square. A channel of water flowed through the middle of these streets, widening into a tank in the middle of the courtyard. The rooms on either side of the arcaded streets were occupied by various officials connected to the fort. The street on the right led eventually to the other main entrance to the fort, the Delhi gate, so named because it faced the older cities of Delhi as opposed to this, Shahjahanabad. This was probably an entrance reserved for the inhabitants of the fort. It was used for instance by the emperor when he went to the congregational mosque in the city, the Jama Masjid. This was also the entrance where the covered carriages of the ladies passed. They would not have used the main visitors' entrance, which is incidentally the only reason why our imaginary visitor has been given a male identity.

The question that immediately occurs of course is, where did all these buildings go? They were all there till the late 1850s, and in fact by that time many more had been added and the fort had become quite full. After the uprising of 1857, when the British army occupied the fort, a vast majority of the buildings were demolished. Part of the space that was freed up was then used in the 1860s to build barracks for the use of the army. These **barracks (3)** can still be seen to your left as you emerge from the Chhatta bazaar.

'After passing into the citadel through this gate (Delhi gate), there is seen a long and spacious street, divided in the midst by a canal of running water. The street has a long divan, or raised way ... It is upon this long divan that all the collectors of market dues and other petty officers exercise their functions.' (Francois Bernier, *Travels in the Mogul Empire, 1656–68*)

4

'In this place ...
in the night,
particularly, when in
bed and afar, on my
terrace this music
sounds in my ears
as solemn, grand
and melodious.'
(Francois Bernier,
*Travels in the Mogul
Empire*, 1656–68)

Across from the Chhatta bazaar, at the eastern end of the imaginary courtyard in which you have been standing is the **Naubat Khana** or **Naqqar Khana (4)**, the drum house. From here the visitor to Shahjahan's court would have proceeded on foot, and today, this is where your ticket is checked before you can go further. In Shahjahan's time this is where the ceremonial drums would have been housed, and played three to five times a day, depending on whether the emperor was in the fort or not. The musicians would have sat in the large open gallery at the top of the building— the part that is now enclosed with windows. The building of the Naqqar Khana is not overly opulent but it has some nice, low relief carving. Particularly see the floral motifs in the many red sandstone panels. The flowers and leaves look realistic but they were to some extent stylized by the artists.

Once through the Naqqar Khana, our seventeenth-century visitor would have found himself in yet another courtyard,

nearly 170 metres from north to south, and over 90 metres from east to west. This courtyard too was surrounded by an arcade of many rooms, and some of these were occupied by lesser nobles who mounted a guard in rotation in the fort. To the north of this courtyard, not visible to the visitor, was the imperial kitchen. To the south, again out of sight, were the private areas of the fort where most of the members of the extended royal family—women, men and children, lived.

The focus of the visitor however would be on what he saw to the east, in his direct line of vision as he emerged through the Naqqar khana. Here, still standing, is the **Diwan-e-Aam (5)**, the hall of public audience. It is a large and beautiful building. In particular, note the red sandstone pillars, and the typically Shahjahani 'cusped' or 'scalloped' arches. The beauty is not so much in the intricacy of detail but in the clean flowing lines of the very stylized foliage that encases the pillar bases and capitals. There are images and descriptions of the Diwan-e-Aam from the early nineteenth century which show all the pillars actually covered in painted and gilded limestone plaster.

At the eastern end of the hall is the white marble throne of the emperor, under a canopy with a 'bangla' or curved roof. Bangla was an adjective applied to roofs that were inspired

'Immediately under the throne is an enclosure, surrounded by silver rails, in which are assembled the whole body of Omrahs (nobility), the Rajas, and the Ambassadors, all standing, their eyes bent downward, their hands crossed. ...the whole courtyard, is filled with persons of all ranks, high and low, rich and poor.' (Francois Bernier, *Travels in the Mogul Empire*, 1656–68)

by Bengali huts. In fact the term later came to be used for a number of different kinds of buildings and evolved into the word 'bungalow'. The throne is quite ornately carved and inlaid with semi-precious stones; and behind it is one of the most fascinating walls in all of Mughal architecture. It is inlaid with a large number of panels, each painstakingly made up by a technique known as 'pietre dure' or small pieces of hard, coloured stones, cut and inlaid to form complex designs. In this case these are images of birds, flowers, lions, and even a panel showing the Greek God Orpheus playing the lute. Some of these panels were imported from Italy and others created by Mughal artists and craftsmen.

The scheme of this wall is a sharp contradiction to the Islamic injunction against the representation of birds, beasts and human beings in pictures as this is considered to be dangerously close to idolatry. One explanation, subscribed to by historians of architecture, is that these considerations were over-ridden by the symbolic content of what was being conveyed to those who saw this court. The realm ruled over by Shahjahan was a paradise; the concept of paradise as a garden being reinforced by the foliage on the pillars, and by the flowers, birds and animals depicted in the inlays. Even more specifically the reign of Shahjahan was like the reign of Solomon, the Islamic ideal of the just king. The imagery of Orpheus playing to the beasts was intended to depict the peaceaful reign of Solomon, where predator and prey were reconciled, and all were safe from oppression. The status of the emperor was further emphasized by the name given to the throne platform—Nasheman-e-Zill-e-Ilahi or 'the seat of the shadow of God'.

We do not know how much of this our seventeenth century visitor understood or even got close enough to see. The emperor sat on a seat placed under the canopy, with his sons standing on either side of him. On the large marble platform at the lower level stood his wazir, who passed on the petitions received in court to his majesty. A wider area around this core was demarcated by railings, within which stood noblemen, feudatories of the empire and ambassadors, but all with their eyes downcast. The rest of the hall was occupied by officials of a fairly high order. Outside the Diwan-e-Aam proper, in the space just in front of it was an area enclosed with red sandstone railings known as the Gulal Bari or red enclosure, where minor officials stood. Outside this stood such of the general populace as got to enter the darbar at all.

The business of court over, the emperor would have left the Diwan-e-Aam through a door set in the wall behind the throne. This took him, through the rooms behind, into an enclosed private courtyard, with a beautiful pool in the middle. Across this courtyard stood the emperor's principal palace—the **Imtiyaz Mahal** or 'palace of distinction', now more popularly known as the **Rang Mahal (6)**, or 'palace of colour'. This building, like the Diwan-e-Aam, is essentially a large pillared hall, with smaller partly enclosed rooms at the northern and southern ends. This open pavilion design was quite flexible and practical. Heavy drapes could be hung to give privacy or protection from the cold and wind. Split bamboo screens, called chik, could provide shade against the sun, without completely blocking out the air and light. And screens of khas (a kind of fine grass), when sprayed with water, would cool the air passing through them.

Of course when the days became unbearably hot there was the option of retreating to the basement, which runs along the length of the building—you can see the apertures of its upper part on the western side. Basements such as this were built precisely for this purpose, as they were cooler than the rooms above which were exposed to the sun.

The Rang Mahal was beautifully decorated. The plastered surface of the upper walls and pillars was covered with painted and gilded patterns. Some of it is has survived in the undersides of the arches. The ceiling of the main hall was originally made of silver, but was removed during the reign of the emperor Farrukhsiyar (1713–19) to be converted into much-needed ready cash. Mirror mosaic, another technique that was popularized by the Mughals is visible in the rooms at either end of the building. Hundreds of tiny pieces of mirror are set in the plaster of the walls to produce an enchanting effect in the light. Rooms with this kind of decoration came to be known as Shish Mahal—'mirror palace'.

An immediately obvious feature of this palace is the water channel running through its length, and forming a beautiful pool in the middle. Water was an important design element in Mughal architecture, and found a place within its buildings as well as in the gardens. A stream of water, an offshoot of a canal that was cut from the Yamuna river somewhat north of Delhi, ran through the gardens and buildings, and was known as the Nahar-e-Bahisht or 'the stream of paradise'. Inside the buildings its effects were ornamental, cooling; and from the sound of the gentle rippling of water, soothing.

The pool in the Rang Mahal is now hard to see because one cannot walk into the hall. It is also damaged, because many of the semi-precious stones used in the floral decoration have been gouged out long ago. We do have descriptions of it which tell us that the rippling water made the flowers and leaves which adorned the bottom of the shallow pool appear to be gently waving in the breeze. Some of the water flowed in a channel to the front of the building, where it cascaded down a section of wall set with many small arched niches. At night these niches held small lamps, and the water flowing in front of them in a thin sheet produced an effect that has been described as 'a quick fall of stars'.

From the level of the Rang Mahal one notable feature of the fort becomes clear: the main buildings are arranged in a row above the eastern wall. This was the side that overlooked the river, and the buildings with their open windows were designed to catch the cooling breeze. The river has now changed its course considerably eastwards, but even in Shahjahan's time there was a wide sandy bank where people of the city would frequently gather for recreation. Royally sponsored elephant fights and kite flying contests

'The young prince led me through different parts of the palace, and I was taken into a superb hall: formerly fountains had played there; the ceiling was painted and inlaid with gold. In this hall were three old women on charpais (native beds), looking like hags ... From a verandah, the young prince pointed out a bastion in which the king was then asleep.'
(Fanny Parks, *Wanderings of a Pilgrim in Search of the Picturesque*, 1838)

also took place here, with the members of the royal family getting a ringside view from their overlooking palaces.

The Rang Mahal is generally described as the palace of the emperor's harem or seraglio—where his wives and/or concubines lived. Some historians however speculate that this was actually the emperor's own private palace. Apart from being conveniently situated just behind the main court of audience, it is located at an important focal point of the fort. It is roughly at the midpoint of the eastern wall which overlooks the river. It is moreover at one end of the axis that leads to the main entrance of the fort and through the main street of the city beyond. Another important clue is the fact that it was frequently described by visitors who, being male, would not have penetrated this far into a building that was primarily occupied by women.

What was definitely a palace for women was the building that is now to the south of the Rang Mahal. This is the **Mumtaz Mahal (7)** or 'eminent palace', also known as the **Chhota Rang Mahal,** or 'small Rang Mahal'. Originally similar in its style of decoration to the Rang Mahal, it has been through many incarnations since 1857—a military prison, a sergeants' mess, and is now the fort museum. The museum has an eclectic collection of artefacts, pictures and documents relating to the fort. The walls of the building still bear some traces of the original decoration.

Remember that much of the area to the south and west of the Mumtaz Mahal, making up about a quarter of the entire area of the fort, was a complex that was the living quarters of the royal family and its attendants. The buildings, courtyards, and gardens are now gone. These have been partly replaced by colonial architecture dating from the British occupation of the mid-nineteenth century.

Go back now past the Rang Mahal to the building just north of it. Known variously as the **Khas Mahal (8)** or 'royal palace', **Baithak** or 'sitting room', **Khwabgah** or 'bedroom', **Tasbih Khana** or a 'room for telling of beads' this has more than one distinct component. In the covered verandah facing the Rang Mahal note the beautifully painted marble surfaces, in particular the subtle colours used. Also note the finely carved filigree of the marble screens and the translucent, carved, marble slabs set in the walls.

Go around to the northern side, and on the way you will see a doorway at the ground level. This led to the riverside, and was the route by which Shahjahan ceremonially entered the fort when it was first inaugurated.

'On passing a screen of Indian connaughts we proceeded to the front of the Tusbeah Khana, and being arrived in the presence of the King, each of us made three obeisances in turn, by throwing down the right hand pretty low, and afterwards raising it to the forehead.' (W. Franklin, *An Account of the Present State of Delhi*, 1801)

Climb up to the plinth of the building on the northern side, and you can see the covered verandah that served as a royal seat. Here the emperor would sit (at least this is what paintings of the nineteenth century show), on furnishings of red and gold, and above him was the carved marble panel depicting the scales of justice. At the eastern end of the rooms, jutting out of the line of the fort wall is an octagonal turret, which is known by its Persian term—Mussamman Burj. Set in this is a jharokha which looks out over what would have been the river bank. This is the Jharokha-e-Darshan, where the emperor showed himself to his subjects every morning so they could reassure themselves that he was alive and well, and be blessed by the vision.

As names and functions have changed over the course of the centuries as it was occupied by various Mughal emperors, we have to make educated guesses as to this building's original function. It certainly seems to have been a more formal building than is suggested by the appellations usually given to it— sitting room, bedroom, prayer room. From their size, location and design these rooms appear to be a sort of private office for the emperor. This was the heart of the empire, where the business of the realm was conducted. Decorative features such as the scales of justice symbolize the ideology of Mughal rule. Long inscriptions over the arches in the inner rooms record the important dates in the history of the fort, including the laying of the foundation, and the inauguration.

To the north of the Khas Mahal is one of the most magnificent buildings of the fort, the **Diwan-e-Khas (9)**, or the 'hall of private audience'. This is where the emperor held a more exclusive court with important ambassadors, courtiers and officials of the realm. This pavilion building too, like the Diwan-e-Aam, was set in a courtyard of its own that was demarcated by a row of arcaded buildings. While the emperor entered the Diwan-e-Khas through the Khas Mahal, most of those who attended the court came from the western side. Our visitor would come past the Diwan-e-Aam, through a passage that connected it to the courtyard of the Diwan-e-Khas, without even a glimpse of the Rang Mahal and the Khas Mahal. He would enter the Diwan-e-Khas courtyard through the door in western wall, which was hung with a red curtain, literally 'lal parda', and from this point he would have to bow and make salutations to the throne as he approached it. He would see, as much as his respectfully lowered eyes would allow, a marvellous spectacle.

Though much despoiled and damaged over the centuries, the Diwan-e-Khas is still a beautiful building. The clean lines of the silhouette and the beautifully curving arches and the light chhatris on the corners of the roof give it an overall sense of simple balance. In decorative detail it manages to be opulent and restrained at the same time. In each of the panels inlaid with coloured stones, which cover the pillars, look at the unfussy flowering plant set amidst the floral border. Particularly observe the very Chinese stylized cloud motifs on either side of the plant. These were influences that had come into the art of the Mughals through their Central

'In front about forty yards was the Dewan khass, or throne-room, in which the King was already seated. ... a long lunged crier proclaimed that we came to see the "King of the World". (A description of the British Commander-in-Chief's visit to Akbar II in 1828, from Major Archer, *Tours in Upper India*)

Asian heritage. The upper part of the pillars and the ceiling are beautifully painted. On a section of one pillar capital in the south-western part of the building, the gilding has been restored to show what it all must originally have looked like. The floor of this building was in its heyday covered with rich carpets, and a bright red awning provided additional shade on all sides of the building.

The opulence of this court was crowned by the famed peacock throne that was placed on a marble platform in the eastern part of the hall. Made of precious metals and studded with an incredible number of precious stones, this was a legendary piece of furniture. It was only too likely to excite avarice and unsurprisingly formed part of the treasure taken away by the Persian ruler Nadir Shah when he extracted a tribute from the prostrate empire in 1739. Nadir Shah had it broken up and the jewels re-used. While it was still in Delhi and in use, it helped to underline the reputation

of the emperor, in the words of contemporary Europeans as 'The Great Mogul'. This epithet was used for instance, by John Dryden as the title of his play about Aurangzeb. A well-known Persian verse of the fourteenth-century Delhi poet Amir Khusro is inscribed over the arches on the inside of the southern and northern walls of the Diwan-e-Khas. In translation it reads: 'If there is paradise on the face of the earth, it is this, it is this, it is this.'

These strong statements of Mughal majesty had to be symbolically countered by the British when they occupied the fort in 1857. It was to strike at the very heart of the aura of Mughal sovereignty when the British captured the fort in September 1857, after suppressing the rebellion in Delhi, that the health of Queen Victoria was toasted in this room. Soon after, it was again in this room that the last emperor Bahadur Shah was tried and sentenced to exile in Rangoon, in what was then Burma.

Next to the Diwan-e-Khas, but sadly out of bounds for visitors, is the **Hammam (10)**. It is a complex building with pools, provision for hot and cold water, steam rooms, and some particularly interesting features such as a basin for a rose water spray. The rooms are lavishly decorated with stone inlay. Take a peek through the window, and you should be able to see some of this. Particularly note the floor. Since this was one building that did not have carpets, the floor was decorated to practically look like one. The hammam was more than a utilitarian area for washing the body. The emperor relaxed here and often conferred with close courtiers too.

11

West of the hammam is another building that is kept locked up. This is the mosque known as **Moti Masjid (11)**, or 'pearl mosque'. Built by Shahjahan's son Aurangzeb, it is made entirely of marble. You can get a glimpse of the interior through a window. There is a fair amount of lavish carving. The floor is marked out in individual panels, each in the shape and size of a mosalla or prayer carpet. The mosque was for private everyday use within the fort, with the emperor going occasionally to the large congregational mosque, the Jama Masjid, in the city. The Moti Masjid originally had copper domes, which were badly damaged by shelling during the British attack on the fort in 1857. They were later rebuilt in marble.

12

North of the Hammam is a small marble pavilion known as **Hira Mahal (12)** or the 'diamond palace'. This was built during the time of Bahadur Shah and it modest size is proof of the meagre resources of the last in line to an illustrious dynasty. There were other buildings in this line along the wall but they were demolished after 1857.

13

North of the Hira Mahal is a beautiful marble pavilion, the main feature of which is a water chute, the head of the Nahar-e-Bahisht, the water channel that ran through the buildings of the fort. This pavilion takes its name from the structure behind it, the **Shah Burj (13)**, or literally the 'royal tower'. This tower, located at the junction of the eastern and northern walls of the fort, was originally three-storeys tall. It was much damaged in 1857, later rebuilt, and is really of not much interest now. As originally built however, it contained an elaborate hydraulic system which controlled

the circulation of water within the fort buildings through a complex system of valves. The water presumably was pumped up from the river in the days when the river was closer. Later, in the nineteenth century, the channel that flowed through the city of Shahjahanabad then passed through the fort. Notice the vaulted roof of this building as this is also a bangla roof such as the one over the throne inside the Diwan-e-Aam.

The garden to the west of these northern buildings is known as **Hayat Baksh Bagh (14)**, 'life-giving garden'. It is now very unlike a traditional Mughal garden. In Shahjahan's times, a garden implied shade-giving, fruit and flowering trees and bushes. Expanses of lawn, which soak up water and give little in return, are not practical in the north Indian climate. The present sensibilities, as reflected in the layout of the garden today, can be dated to British colonial times, when the administrators sought to recreate the grassy look of their own homeland.

15

Sawan (15) at the northern end and **Bhadon (16)** on the southern end are the only two marble buildings that remain today from the original layout of the garden. The names are those of the two rainy months of the monsoon season, and the emphasis in the design of both these buildings was on water. Note the water channel that would have water travelling across the floor and falling in a sheet in front of the rows of small niches, which contained flower vases during the day and lamps at night.

17

The two pavilions were meant to face each other across the garden with a large tank of water in the middle, but here Bahadur Shah built the red sandstone pavilion called **Zafar Mahal (17)**. Nothing much is to be said about this, but note the extremely slender pillars that are a feature of late Mughal architecture.

SHAHJAHANABAD

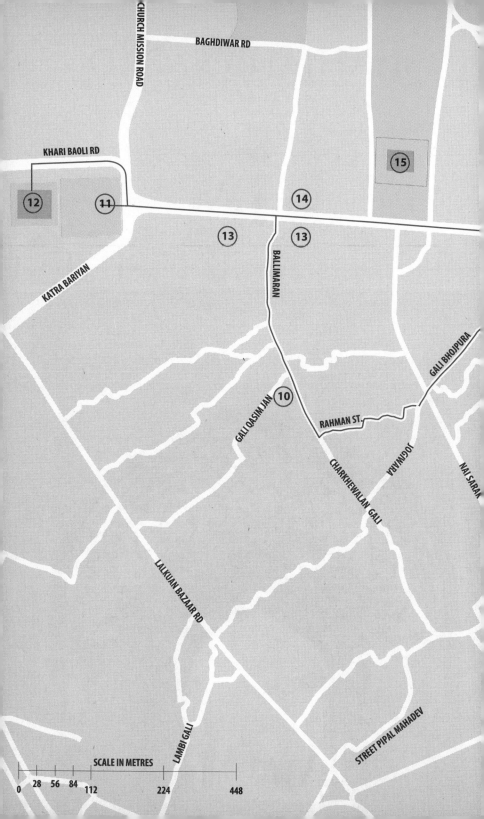

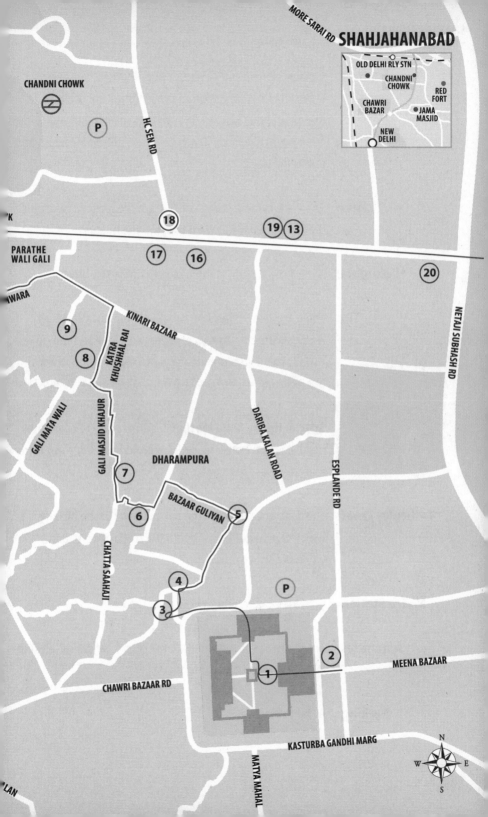

Timings: Mostly open during daylight hours all week. Jama Masjid is closed to casual visitors at prayer times, particularly mid-day, about 12.15–1.45 p.m. The Ghalib memorial is open every day from 10 a.m. to 5 p.m. except Mondays and public holidays.

Tickets: There is a camera charge of ₹200 at the Jama Masjid, plus a small charge if you want to climb the minaret.

Highlights: Jama Masjid, Naya Mandir, Meru Mandir, Naughara.

Tip: There are Jain temples on this route. You must leave all leather garments and accessories outside when you go in. Usually there is someone who will look after your things but it is a good idea to take along a cloth bag for valuables.

Special tip for Jama Masjid: It is customary to cover the head. It is also better to avoid wearing shorts or short skirts and sleeveless garments.

Difficulty Level: The walk goes through the narrow lanes of the old city, which can be quite crowded particularly after 10 a.m. when the shops open.

Metro Station: Chawri Bazaar on the Yellow line, 0.75 km.

Amenities: There are small restaurants and eating places all around, including famous street food.

Parking: At Jama Masjid.

IMPERIAL CITY

It was about 1639 that the Mughal emperor Shahjahan decided to build a new capital at Delhi —Shahjahanabad ('founded by Shahjahan'). Over the next few years, attention and resources were completely focussed on the palace complex that would be built within it or what we today know of as the Red Fort. It was only in 1648 that the city began to be built. In shape it was roughly semicircular, or bow-shaped, with the straight or 'string' side towards the river on the east. Its perimeter wall was more than 6 kms in length, and punctuated by thirteen gates and numerous small wicket gates.

The middle half of the river front was occupied by the fort, and around the fort on the remaining sides lay the city. One broad street stretched from the western or Lahore gate of the fort right through the city. This is what we today call Chandni Chowk. Another street, known as Faiz Bazaar, led from the southern or Delhi gate of the fort to the Delhi Gate of the city through Daryaganj. Finally, one shorter street led from the southern gate of the fort to the main congregational mosque of the city—the Jama Masjid ('jama' being congregation).

Imperial planning went no further than the fort, the city wall, some main

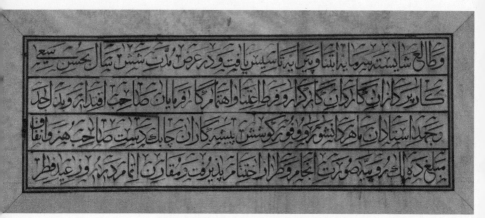

streets and landmarks like the Jama Masjid. The remaining spaces were filled in through individual enterprise. Some of these were by the members of the royal family—two of the emperor's wives built mosques, his favourite daughter, Jahanara, laid out a large garden. The rich set up estates which housed their own mansions and gardens, their considerable domestic staff and often small manufacturing units for the needs of the household. There were entrepreneurs who built markets, many built places of worship, and finally the mass of the population built their own more modest houses.

The city has changed considerably in the more than 350 years since it was first established. The change started quite early. One of the first signs of decline in the Mughal Empire, which set in by the middle of the eighteenth century, was the fading fortunes of the noble families. Over time the large estates were sold and/or partitioned, and denser neighbourhoods grew up in their place. These were not exactly poor settlements as the eighteenth century was by no means a time of unmitigated decline. Mercantile groups still flourished and in fact there was a flurry of building activity, particularly of temples and mosques, but also of markets and houses.

A major change came after 1857. The uprising against British rule and its brutal suppression by the British armed forces was a traumatic episode in the history of the city. In its aftermath came a deliberate destruction of many buildings in the city. Some of it was an ostensibly defensive measure—to clear a hundred yard swathe of land around the Red Fort, which was now occupied by British troops. Some it was a symbolic replacement of Mughal structures with typically British colonial ones—like the Town Hall and Clock tower. And finally, the railway was driven through the heart of the city, destroying many buildings in the northern half of Shahjahanabad.

Today Shahjahanabad is a bustling place. Its narrow streets are crowded with people going about their business—and a lot of this is commercial activity in wholesale markets and small workshops. But despite the crowds and the less-than-clean lanes, it has its charm—in the unexpectedly beautiful building façades and balconies, the colourful markets, and the street food. In the age of isolated and climate-controlled shopping malls, daily life here still goes on at street level.

THE WALK

1

Begin at the major landmark of Shahjahanabad—**Jama Masjid (1)**. This was the congregational mosque of the city, and was built on a natural rise in the ground, called Bhojla Pahar. The foundation was laid on 6 October 1650 and it took six years to build at the cost of ₹1,000,000 at the time. The Jama Masjid represents a high point in Mughal architecture. The shape and proportions of the gateways, the western façade, domes and minarets attain a perfection that spawned many copies but was never entirely successfully replicated.

The eastern entrance faces the Delhi gate of the Red Fort and was the royal entrance, through which the emperor would enter in state. This broad street, just under a kilo-

metre long, was lined by shops that made up the Khas Bazaar. There are entrances on the southern and northern sides of the mosque too. All these entrances are reached by broad steps and this was a busy social space though much of the city's past. The steps were crowded with hawkers and street food vendors, jugglers and storytellers. Particularly in the evenings, this was the place to be. The famous eighteenth century Delhi poet, Mir, is believed to have said that to understand his poetry it was essential to be familiar with the steps of the Jama Masjid! Today the steps are generally emptier, but particularly on festivals, the congregation in the mosque spills over onto the steps. The markings in white paint demarcate standing and kneeling space for each person.

As you begin to climb the steps of the eastern gate, on your right you will see the **shrine of Sarmad Shaheed (2)**. Sarmad was an interesting person, Jewish and from Armenia (some say Iran). He was a successful trader but while on trip to Sindh he converted to Islam and also became attracted to mysticism. He distanced himself from worldly concerns, his asceticism even leading him to discard his clothes. After travelling around for a while he came to Delhi, where Shahjahan's son, Dara Shikoh, himself interested in mysticism and with an unorthodox approach to religion in general, became his disciple. Dara Shikoh however was put to death on the orders of his brother Aurangzeb in a tussle over succession, and Sarmad wound up on the wrong side of the political divide. His unorthodox ways gave Aurangzeb ample ammunition against him. Sarmad's nudity was one charge against him. The other was that when asked to

recite the Islamic creed—'There is no God but God and Mohammad is his Prophet', he stopped short at 'there is no God', saying that in his attempt to understand the mysteries of God he had so far only got to this stage.

Sarmad was found guilty of heresy and beheaded at the orders of the emperor. The story of his death itself is interesting and has two versions. One is that as soon as his head hit the ground, the full kalima was spoken from his mouth, and the head rolled the distance from the palace to the Jama Masjid reciting praises of God. The other version is that the headless body picked up the head and started to walk towards the mosque in anger. As he reached the foot of the steps, the voice of his spiritual master Syed Hare Bhare Shah, who was buried there, was heard to ask 'where are you going?' When Sarmad replied that he was going to lay his case before God, Hare Bhare Shah persuaded him to give up his anger as he had reached his destination. Sarmad's body collapsed right there, and he was buried at that spot. The interior of the shrine is painted red. Next to it is the shrine of Hare Bhare Shah.

Now climb the steps, leave your shoes outside and enter the large courtyard of the mosque. The inside of each entrance way is beautifully made of red sandstone. The eastern or 'royal' gateway has a beautiful jharokha above the central arch. Along the top is a row of kanguras. The other gates are nice too; look at the row of miniature chhatris along the top. The arched, open verandahs that run along three sides of the courtyard are a perfect design element— they are open so they give a view out over the city and the fort, at the same time they provide a covered space that can be used for various purposes, especially as a resting place. Look at the large chhatris that add a neat finish to the corners of the courtyard.

The pool of water in the courtyard is the traditional wuzu tank. This provides water for the ritual ablutions that precede prayer. Now of course water is also provided via taps set up elsewhere. In the north-western corner of the tank is a small spot that has been marked off with a low marble railing. Mohammad Khan Tahsin, an important eunuch in charge of the royal harem, saw the Prophet Mohammad standing at this spot in a dream. This took place in the year 1180 of the Hijri calendar, corresponding to 1766–67.

In front of the pool is a small beige sandstone kiosk. This was put up in about 1829 by Mirza Salim the son of the emperor Akbar II, to serve as a pulpit for the mukabbir, who follows the imam's movements of prayer, for the benefit of those in the courtyard who cannot see the imam himself.

On the western side of the courtyard is the qibla which is marked out by a façade of arches, behind which there is a covered area. This shape of arch— with little scallops coming to a point at the top, is a particular feature of Mughal architecture from Shahjahan onwards. The inscriptions in black marble inlaid on the white marble panels above the arches, talk in hyperbolic terms of Shahjahan and the building of the mosque. The central arch simply has two circular medallions on which is written in Arabic, 'O Guide!'— one of the ninety-nine names of Allah.

'If you want to know what the vault and cupola of its prayer chamber are like, nothing can be said except (that they resemble) the milky way and sky. The dome would have been matchless had the firmament not been its equal, the vault would have been unique had the milky way not been its pair.' (Inscription on one of the arches of the façade of the Jama Masjid.)

185

At the foot of the central arch is another kiosk meant for the mukabbir, built in 1928. Climb on to the covered area of the mosque. Notice that the floor is divided by lines of inlaid black marble into rectangles that mimic the shape of the mosalla. There are 899 of these. The minbar beside the central mihrab is believed to be carved out of a single piece of marble.

It is easy to recognize heritage buildings in Shahjahanabad from the iron sign boards that stand before most, proclaiming them as such.

The Jama Masjid, being the main congregational mosque of the city, was under the direct management of the Mughal emperor who appointed its important functionaries such as the imam. After quelling the uprising of 1857 and capturing Delhi, the British confiscated the mosque and quartered soldiers there. For a while there was also talk of destroying the mosque altogether as a punishment for the people of Delhi. There were others who were opposed to this and so the mosque survived. Another royal mosque close by— Akbarabadi masjid, built by a wife of Shahjahan, was not so fortunate. It was only in 1862, after much negotiation, that the Jama Masjid was handed back to the Muslims of Delhi. Shockingly, one of the conditions was that Europeans would be allowed to enter it without taking off their shoes!

Leave the mosque by the northern gateway. Cross the street outside and go a little way to the left, to the corner formed by the row of buildings that line the large square surrounding the mosque. In the corner is the **Indraprastha Girls School (3)**. Founded in 1904, it is one of the earliest schools for girls in Delhi. Before this was established, girls were invariably taught at home. The building is a haveli, or a mansion that already existed here when the school was

founded. It is a well kept building as is obvious even from the outside. The inside is equally interesting, though it is usually not possible to visit it.

Come back from the school and take the first turning to the left, into a narrow passageway. On the left, this is bounded by a high old wall and as you emerge into the open, on your left is what remains of the **Chah Rahat (4)**, or the 'well with the Persian wheel', which supplied water to the Jama Masjid. A Persian inscription written on a stone slab set in the wall tells you just that.

Take the lane going north (known as Chah Rahat) and you will find crumbling old buildings, particularly on the left. This area is all that remains of one of the original large estates of Shahjahanabad. It belonged to Ustad Hamid, a master builder, who was responsible for the construction of the Red Fort. In time the estate broke up and the plot was divided up to hold independently owned buildings. At its end you will pass through a gateway, which is probably all that remains of the original structures of the estate. This is called the gateway of **Kucha Ustad Hamid (5)**. Kucha means lane; so the name of Ustad Hamid still survives in the name of the street.

From the gateway of Kucha Ustad Hamid turn left and proceed a little way down. This is known as bazaar Gulian. Go past the first lane to the left and turn left into the second. You are now in an area called Dharampura. Walk a little way down this lane until you come to a lane to your right. At the corner of these two lanes, at the first floor level you will

The lanes of Shahjahanabad can be confusing. Shops however, often have names of streets written on them, and you can ask to verify that you are on the right track.

6

see an ornately carved building. This is the **Digambar Jain Naya Mandir (6)**. The Jains have been an important religious sect in Delhi for many centuries. The Digambars are one of the two main divisions of the Jains (the Swetambars being the other). In the times of the Mughals, the Jains were important merchants and bankers, who played a crucial role in provisioning the royal armies and otherwise financing the business of empire. A part of their wealth went towards financing many temples in the city. This is particularly true of Dharampura.

The temple is called Naya Mandir, which means 'new temple' but it was actually built in 1807, which amply illustrates the

problem of naming anything 'new'—with any luck it's bound to get old! It has some lovely carving on the outside, in beige sandstone. Look at the curving brackets that support the kiosk on top of the doorway. It is worth going inside and up to the first floor, if just to see the beautifully painted ceilings. The room adjoining the courtyard, is done in nice colours and is reminiscent of the style used in the Red Fort whereas the one in the inner shrine is extremely rich and ornate.

As you leave the Naya Mandir, take the lane that passes in front of it. It will take you to a doorway, which makes you think you are entering someone's house. Persevere. It is a thoroughfare, which will bring you out to a street known as Gali Masjid Khajur. It has some nice gateways, finely carved in sandstone. Turn right onto it and soon on your right you will see an elaborate gateway with a projecting balcony over it. This is the **Digambar Jain Meru Mandir (7)**. Built in the mid-eighteenth century, this is a temple worth a visit. It is less touristy than some other Jain temples, and there has been relatively less alteration and painting-over. There are interesting images and paintings inside, particularly a room which has a number of pedestals with little idols on top.

Continue up the street and it will come to an end; turn left and soon after, right. This lane is Katra Khushhal Rai, and soon after on your left will be the haveli or house known as **Shish Mahal (8)**. This is a modestly-sized town house and you can step inside. The rooms are arranged around a central courtyard, originally only on two storeys. This building also has an interesting association. This is where St Stephen's College, one of the better-known colleges of the country, had its humble beginnings in 1881.

Katra Khushhal Rai ends up in the busy Kinari Bazaar. This is a street specializing in gilt laces and other similar accessories and raw materials suitable for weddings and festivals. It is bright and colourful and often full of tourists in rickshaws.

9

Turn left into it, and then left shortly after into a cul de sac called **Naughara (9)** or literally, 'nine houses'. This is a surprisingly tranquil residential street, with a row of house fronts on the right. Most of them are now painted in a variety of colours, but the base is the same sandstone you see on haveli façades throughout the city. On the left, behind an old doorway with a pointed arch is the common open area that was shared by these households. At the end of the cul de sac is a Jain temple called Jauhri mandir, literally 'jewellers' temple' after its patrons. It is said that this temple existed here even in the time of Shahjahan, though the visible parts of it have obviously been rebuilt. It is quite opulent and also very well visited by tourists. Much of the ornamentation is quite recent.

Kinari Bazaar continues in a north-westerly direction until it meets up with two other lanes, forming a tiraha or tri-junction. On the right is **Parathe wali gali**. This is famous for its roadside eateries serving deep fried parathas (breads) with an unusual variety of fillings. On the left is the road called Maliwara. Take this and walk on it for a while. It will intersect with Nai Sadak or 'new road', built in the 1860s. Cross Nai Sadak and continue a short way down Maliwara, then take the first turning to the right. Move in a south-westerly direction, down this very winding street and it will open into a broad street called Ballimaran.

Ballimaran is very well known so you can ask people to direct you to it. Alternatively there is a more straightforward way to get there from Maliwara. Don't take the turning to the right after you cross Nai Sadak, but continue on the

Maliwara road. When you come to a branch take the right. This will bring you to Ballimaran; turn right into it.

There is some controversy about the name Ballimaran. Most say it refers to the makers of 'ballis' or oars. One source from the nineteenth century (a letter from the poet Ghalib) suggests that the word might actually have been 'Billi-maran', referring to the killers of cats! More than cats or oars however, Ballimaran has been known historically for its hakims or doctors of the system of medicine called Yunani. Yunani literally means Greek and it was an ancient system picked up by the Arabs from the Greek tradition and then disseminated further around the world.

The best-known family of hakims in Ballimaran is the Sharif Khani family, whose members were physicians to the Mughal emperors. One member of the family—Hakim Ajmal Khan was a noted nationalist leader. As you make your way up Ballimaran, you will find the lane called Gali Qasim Jan on your left. This is a short distance if you came via the winding shortcut from Maliwara, somewhat longer if you took the longer route.

On Gali Qasim Jan, one of the first important buildings to the left is the **haveli of Mirza Ghalib (10)**. It is entered through a semicircular arch made out of brick, and there is a small memorial inside it. Acknowledged as one of India's greatest Persian and Urdu poets, Ghalib lived in Delhi from his early teens, or about 1810 onwards. In the nineteenth century the Mughal emperor was an impecunious pensioner of the British, and the traditional nobility was also

in decline. Ghalib therefore was perennially short of patrons and funds to support his fairly lavish lifestyle, which was dictated by his inherited noble status. He never owned a house and moved several times, from one rented place to another. This house belonged to one of the hakims, and he lived here towards the end of his life. Only a small part of the house— much modified, is the memorial.

Come back to Ballimaran and proceed further on it, till it opens on to a very broad street— Chandni Chowk. Turn left and walk till you come to the end, at which you will find **Fatehpuri masjid (11)**. This mosque was built in 1650 by one of the wives of Shahjahan, Fatehpuri begum or 'the lady from Fatehpur'. It is smaller but in some essentials similar to the Jama Masjid. It has a particularly tranquil atmosphere. The several graves in the courtyard belong to people who

have been associated with the mosque. If you go outside the southern gateway of the mosque you can see on the first floor the Mughal building of the library and the adjoining British colonial style building of a school.

This mosque too was confiscated by the British government after the uprising of 1857. The surrounding arcade, which had shops on the outside, was sold to a Hindu entrepreneur of the city—Lala Chunna Mal. This decision was reversed many years later, in 1877, when Chunna Mal was compensated with land elsewhere and the mosque was returned in its entirety to the Muslims of the city.

Leave the mosque by the eastern gate (remember the domed area across the courtyard denotes west), and walk around the shops to go to the northern side of the mosque—you will be taking a left from the exit and a left again. You are now in Khari Baoli, named after a now non-existent brackish well. This is a fascinating wholesale spice market. Go past the northern entrance to the mosque and the next broad gateway to your left leads into the **Gadodia market building (12)**. Built in the early twentieth century,  this three-storeyed building has rooms arranged around a large courtyard, which unfortunately has now been built on too. The best way to see the mixed architecture of the building is to go to the top via the stairs to the left, a little inside the entrance. The top also gives you a good view of the Fatehpuri Masjid, which is immediately to the east; and beyond it down the length of Chandni Chowk, the street that leads to the Red Fort. A bit to the right you can find the domes and minarets of the Jama Masjid in your view too.

'... the narrow counters, so gorgeous with silks and brocades and heavy embroideries, so tempting and so costly ... the broad avenue, with its umbrageous trees ... the glaring lights, the masses of colour, the noise and the hubbub, the raucous conversation in stentorian tones.' (Lovat Fraser, *At Delhi*, 1902)

Descend and go back to the front of the Fatehpuri Masjid. Now if you are really tired, you can take one of the small, battery-operated buses that carry you down Chandni Chowk or you can take a rickshaw, which will give you a better view. Or you might feel energetic enough to walk, which will give you the most leisurely view of the street. If you do this, keep to the pavement on the left.

The street now known as Chandni Chowk, in its heyday was even wider than it is today. It had a channel of water running down its middle, and shady trees on either side. Shops, with the fronts shaded by awnings, lined either side. The water channel was supplied by an offshoot from what is known as the Western Yamuna Canal, a major irrigation canal. An uneven supply in the canal led to drying up of this channel from time to time particularly, if nothing was actively done to keep it open. Finally in late nineteenth century it was decided to close up the channel completely and in the early twentieth century a tramline was started in the middle of the road. This was discontinued in 1963.

As you walk down Chandni Chowk you can take in some of the sights on either side of the road. To the right are some early twentieth century bank buildings with delight-fully flamboyant and eclectic façades—look particularly at the fussy but charming grill-work. Some of the best build-ings on the street are actually **bank buildings (13)**. Then to the left is a long two-storeyed building with a verandah running its length, on the first floor. The ground floor is occupied by shops. This is the **haveli of Chunna Mal (14)**, whom we met earlier in the Fatehpuri Masjid. Chunna Mal

speculated in the fluid property market in the years after 1857, and did very well out of it. This enabled him to build this grand building with this unusually broad frontage on the main street.

A short walk from this the road opens up into a square, which is the original 'chandni chowk' or 'moonlit square'. In the days of Shahjahan this square had a pool of water in the middle, which prettily reflected the moonlight, hence the name. To the south (now to your right) was a hammam. To the north (now on your left) was the entrance to a large garden laid out by Shahjahan's daughter Jahanara, and called Begum ka Bagh or 'garden of the lady'. The garden contained several buildings too, including a sarai. In 1857, this was confiscated by the British government like all the other royal properties. The gardens were relaid in a colonial style and named Queen's Gardens. The buildings were demolished and a new building, which soon became the **Town Hall (15)**, was built. You can still see this on your left,

though the statue of Queen Victoria has been replaced by that of Swami Shraddhanand, the noted nationalist and Arya Samaj leader.

The bathhouses at the southern end of the chowk were also demolished and a new road was built through this area—the Nai Sadak, which we encountered earlier. The pool of water was replaced by a typically Victorian clock tower, which stood there until 1951 when one morning it came crashing down and was never rebuilt.

The next busy square on this street is called Bhai Mati Das Chowk, but was originally called Kotwali Chowk or 'the square of the police station'. The southern end of this square

was occupied by the main police authority building of Shahjahanabad during the time of the Mughals, when certain important events took place here. One was the execution in 1675 of Guru Tegh Bahadur, by orders of Emperor Aurangzeb. Tegh Bahadur was the ninth Guru or leader of the Sikhs, who carried on a persistent resistance movement against the Mughal Empire. However, later in the eighteenth century the Sikhs were allowed to build a memorial to the Guru near the spot. The **Gurudwara Sis Ganj (16)** has grown and has acquired the buildings all around, finally pushing out the kotwali itself, the last buildings of which were demolished some decades ago.

To the right of the gurudwara is a mosque that is rather dwarfed by it—**Sunehri Masjid (17)** or golden mosque, so named because of its now rather tarnished copper domes. Built by a nobleman around 1721–22, it has a rather bloody incident associated with its name. In 1739 the Persian invader, Nadir Shah, entered Delhi and the city and the emperor submitted fairly quietly to him, except for an incident when some of his soldiers were killed. This prompted him to order a massacre of the city's population until the then Mughal emperor, Mohammad Shah, literally begged him to stop. It is said that Nadir Shah watched the massacre from the steps of this mosque.

To the north of the square is a fountain, painted white and blue. This is the **Northbrook Fountain (18)**, named after Lord Northbrook, the Viceroy of India (1872–76). This was added to the streetscape of Chandni

Chowk as a colonial 'improvement', to commemorate the visit of the Viceroy.

A little further down, to the left, is the **Central Baptist Church (19)**, built in 1858. It is a rather plain and uninteresting building but is one of the oldest churches in the city. After this, on the other side of the road are two temples— first, the Gauri Shankar temple with its tall white shikhar or spires, and second, the only slightly shorter **Jain Lal Mandir (20)**. This last is the most important of the Jain temples of the city. A Jain shrine existed here even in the time of Shahjahan, though this building dates mostly from the nineteenth century. Attached to it is an interesting bird hospital, run as a charity by the Jains who have a special reverence for the sacredness of all life.

MEHRAULI
VILLAGE

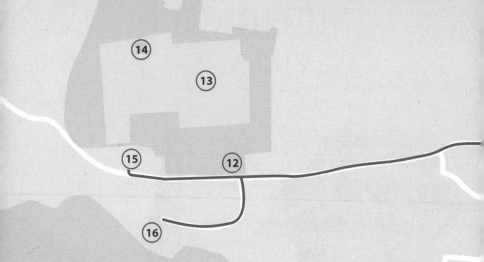

14

13

15   12

16

ANUVRAT MARG

QUTAB MINAR

MEHRAULI VILLAGE

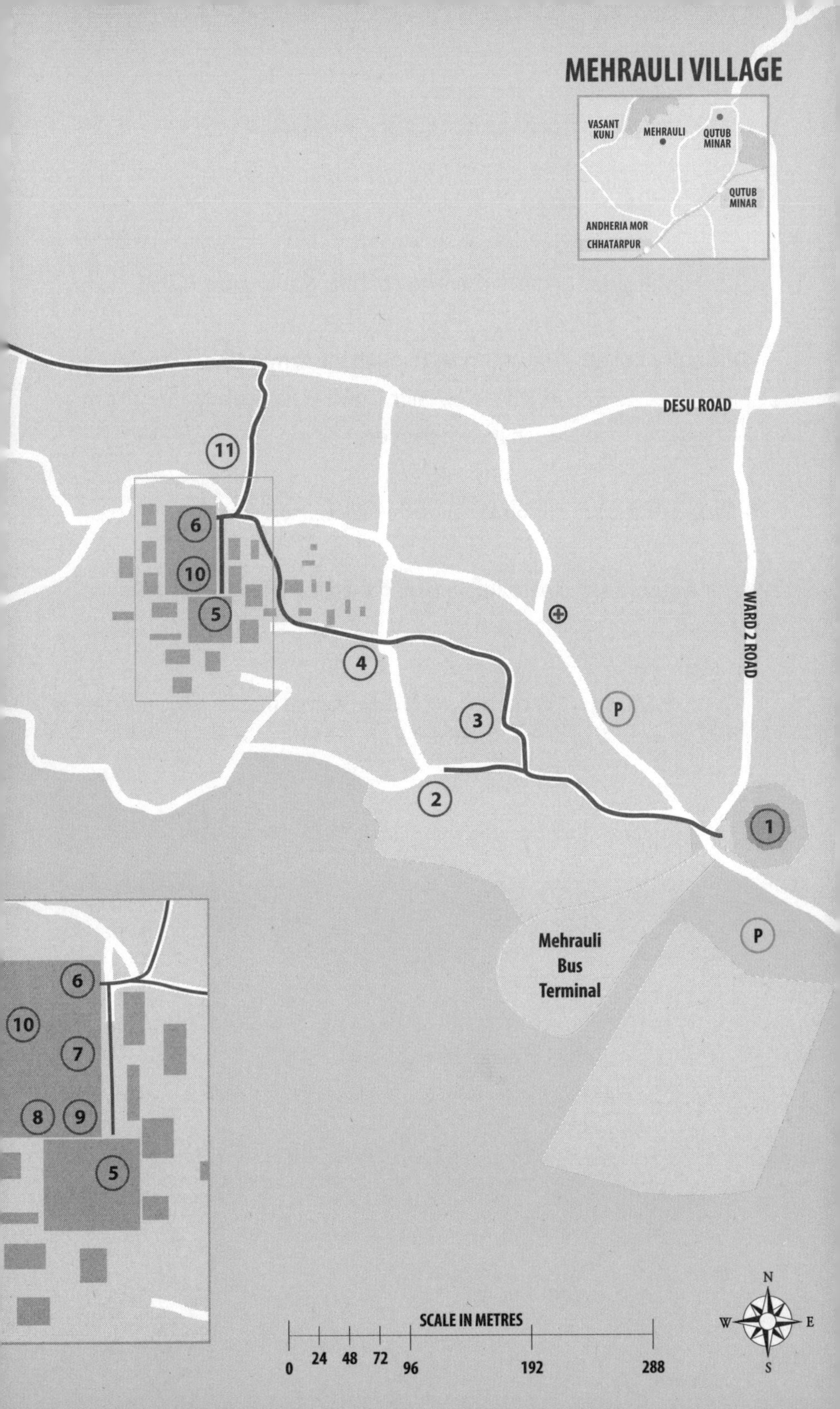

VASANT KUNJ

MEHRAULI

QUTUB MINAR

QUTUB MINAR

ANDHERIA MOR

CHHATARPUR

DESU ROAD

WARD 2 ROAD

11

6

10

5

4

3

2

1

P

P

Mehrauli
Bus
Terminal

6

10

7

8   9

5

SCALE IN METRES

0   24   48   72   96   192   288

N

W   E

S

Timings: Open all day during daylight hours.

Tickets: Free.

Highlights: Adham Khan's tomb, Zafar Mahal, Jahaz Mahal, Jharna.

Difficulty Level: The walk goes through the narrow lanes of the village, which can be quite crowded particularly after 10 a.m. when the shops open.

Metro Station: Qutub Minar on the Yellow line, 2 kms.

Amenities: There are shops and even some quite fancy restaurants in Mehrauli.

Parking: Official parking lot across from the Jog Maya temple.

HISTORIC VILLAGE

Located beside the World Heritage Site of the Qutub Minar, this historic 'urban village' is densely populated with beautiful old buildings, each with fascinating stories and contemporary beliefs and practices attached to them. In the early thirteenth century this settlement began to spread out to the south of Lal Kot, the fortification in which the Qutub Minar is situated. Lal Kot had been established by the Tomar Rajput dynasty in the eleventh century. In the twelfth century, it was expanded into Qila Rai Pithora by their successors, another Rajput clan—the Chauhans. The late twelfth century saw the founding of the Delhi Sultanate or the empire founded by the Turks. They conquered this fortified city from the Chauhans and made it their capital for the next hundred years or more.

As the population grew to the south of Lal Kot, material and cultural infrastructure grew with it—houses, wells, tombs, the seat of a revered Sufi saint, a large water reservoir. Even after the capital of the Sultanate moved away from here and newer cities were established, Mehrauli continued to be populated and thrived reasonably well. The shrine of the saint Qutubuddin Bakhtiyar Kaki continued to thrive and receive visitors from near and far, as did the nearby Hindu temple of the goddess Jog Maya. The belief in the sacred aura of Qutubuddin encouraged burials in the vicinity. There were other spots associated with the early history of Islam in India located here too, and mosques and shrines big and small grew around them.

The topography of the area with its picturesque hilly terrain, the streams and the reservoir made it a popular recreational area too. There was game in the surrounding area as well for the city folk to go hunting. Finally, the micro-climate here was believed to be healthier than in the newer cities such as Shahjahanabad in the north. These factors led the rich to build picturesque country retreats here. A climax in this trend was reached in the early nineteenth century when the last two Mughal emperors, who were nothing more than pensioners of the British East India Company, built a palace complex here and began to regularly spend time in it.

Today, Mehrauli village is a bustling part of the city; a fascinating mix of traditional and modern ways of life.

THE WALK

The walk begins at the **tomb of Adham Khan (1)**, situated prominently on a height near the busy bus terminal. It is also popularly known as **Bhulbhulaiyan** or maze. Adham Khan was the son of Maham Angah, the wet nurse of the Mughal emperor Akbar. There was some amount of rivalry between the family of Maham Angah and that of Jiji Angah, another wet nurse of the emperor. One day in 1862, Adham Khan stabbed to death the husband of Jiji Angah, who went by the title of Atgah Khan. In punishment, Akbar had Adham Khan thrown from the ramparts of the fort at Agra, which was at the time the capital of the Mughal Empire and where these events took place. Adham Khan's body was brought to Delhi, to be buried near the shrine of the revered saint Qutubuddin Bakhtiyar Kaki. Akbar had this grand mauso-

leum built, and when Maham Angah died soon after, she was buried here too.

This eight-sided tomb is built mainly of grey quartzite, widely available in and around Delhi. The upper part of the building is covered with limestone plaster—very sparsely decorated with carved or incised motifs. In the upper part of the building there is a passageway of connected rooms that runs around the central room. The arrangement is confusing as it is not easy to spot the entrance to the steps leading down. This is the reason for this building's popular name—Bhulbhulaiyan or maze. The enclosure in which the tomb is placed is located on a bastion in the thick wall of the ancient city of Lal Kot or 'red fort', so called because of the bricks from which it was originally constructed.

The village of Mehrauli spreads out to the south of Adham Khan's tomb. Upon emerging from the tomb, the steps lead down on to a busy space and a broad road. Ignore the left fork of this road as it leads to a bus terminus, instead take the right, and then take the first turning left. This street leads to the **Gandhak ki baoli (2)**, which you will find within a fenced enclosure on your left. This was a well that was fed by a natural sulphur spring, hence the name 'gandhak' that means sulphur.

This is an old well, dating to the time when Iltutmish, one of the Turkish 'slave sultans' was on the throne (1210–35). The slave sultans are so called because they were technically slaves, purchased when young and raised to be very competent soldiers and administrators. During the early years of the Delhi Sultanate, usually it was a slave who was the nominated successor to the throne of his master. Hence Qutubuddin Aibak followed Mohammad Ghori, and Iltutmish followed Aibak. Anyhow, this makes it one of the oldest step-wells in Delhi.

Turn back from the baoli and go a short way back up the street on which you came, and take the first turning to the left. It is a path winding between various buildings— particularly notice an old Mughal gateway on your left. This is all that is left of the **house of Kale Sahib (3)**, whose real name was Ghulam Nasiruddin. He was a Sufi saint who numbered among his friends and disciples eminent people such as the last Mughal emperors Akbar II and Bahadur Shah, and the poet Ghalib. Though he lived most of the time in Shahjahanabad, like many of the rich people of Delhi he had a second home in Mehrauli.

Ignore the first turning to the left after the gateway, and take the next. Continue southwards on this and you will soon come to two tallish piers of an old gateway known as **Naubat Khana (4)**. This gateway was built as an entrance-way to the shrine of Qutubuddin, also known as Qutub Sahab, during the reign of Sher Shah Sur (1540–45).

The gateway is in a very sad condition now. The gallery has

disappeared. The eastern pier has been taken over by a gurudwara and whitewashed. The western pier at least has signs of its original ornamentation and colour. Look at the beautifully carved brackets that supported the jharokha.

The location of the Naubat Khana tells you that the dargah or shrine must be close, and soon you will come to a busy junction of narrow lanes, on one side of which is the entrance to the shrine. Though this is the more popular way in, it is better for the purposes of this walk to enter through the western entrance further on. So turn right at this point into the very narrow lane and take the first turning to the

left. This will climb for a bit before coming into a somewhat open space. Before you is an imposing gateway, the entrance to Zafar Mahal, but ignore this for now and instead walk through the smaller doorway set to the left. This is the western gateway to **the shrine of Qutub Sahab (5)**. You will have to take off your shoes at some point but it should be possible to carry them with you as long as they are held with the soles against each other.

The shrine complex is a maze of enclosures, mostly occupied by graves. Unlike the Nizamuddin dargah however, these buildings are hardly of significant architectural beauty nor are there particularly famous people buried in this complex.

It does have atmosphere of course and is the shrine of a saint who has great spiritual and historic significance.

Khwaja Qutubuddin Bakhtiyar was born in Osh (now in Kyrgyzstan), but came to India at the time when the Turks first founded the Delhi Sultanate, in the late twelfth century. He became a disciple of Muinuddin Chishti, who founded the Chishtiya Sufi order in India. Muinuddin Chishti, who had his seat in Ajmer, nominated Qutubuddin his spiritual successor and ordered him to go to Delhi. The latter came to Delhi most likely during the reign of Iltutmish. Delhi, under the protection of the Sultanate had become a major centre of Islamic learning, culture and spirituality after the destruction of Central Asian centres by the Mongols under Chengiz Khan.

Women are not permitted to enter the enclosure which contains the grave of the saint. They may look in through the screen windows set into the enclosing wall.

The work and popularity of the saint extended to non-Muslims too, and he and other Sufis won over many Hindu followers. Qutubuddin's popularity meant that he received large donations from the rich, which were then expended in charity. The traveller Ibn Batuta, who visited Delhi about a century after the death of the saint tells us the story behind the nickname of the saint, 'Kaki'. According to him, the saint was frequently visited by those in financial need, and he helped them out by giving them a biscuit or kaka, of gold or silver, and thus came to be known as 'Kaki'. After his death in 1235, his shrine continued to be a popular place of pilgrimage. It still is, and is visited by many, including, non-Muslims, particularly during the annual celebration of the urs. The urs of a saint, literally 'wedding', is the date of his death, the imagery of a wedding symbolizing the union with God.

'The fair at Mehrauli especially is a favourite resort for the Delhi people ... It is called the "Pankha Mela", because "Pankhas" are carried in procession on Wednesday to the Hindu temple, "Jog Maya", and on Thursday to the Kutbdin' (Oswald Wood, *Final report on the settlement of land revenue in the Delhi district*, 1872–77)

You leave the dargah the way you entered, and then visit the complex on the left, which is **Zafar Mahal (6–10)**. It is named after the last Mughal emperor Bahadur Shah 'Zafar' who built the imposing gate, but his father Akbar II had already built substantial portions of the palace. There were good reasons for building a palace in Mehrauli. The later Mughals were devotees of Qutub Sahab, and several members of the family were buried around the shrine. The practice of visiting Mehrauli was also well established, particularly during the monsoon when the nearby tank and streams were full of water and there was plenty of greenery around.

In the year 1811 a new tradition was instituted that strengthened the tie between the Mughal royal family and the shrine. In 1809, Mirza Jahangir, the son of Akbar II, was exiled to Allahabad by the British. His mother Mumtaz Mahal took a vow that she would offer a canopy and coverlet of flowers at the shrine of Qutubuddin Bakhtiyar Kaki if her son returned to Delhi. When he returned, this was done with great pomp. The flower sellers of the city, who were commissioned to prepare the floral offerings, added floral pankhas or fans to the procession on their own accord. This was such a popular event that it immediately became an annual fair sponsored by the palace, and was continued under Bahadur Shah as well. The fair was celebrated each year sometime in the monsoon, the date being fixed by the emperor at the request of the flower sellers. It is still held each year, though now just before winter sets in. It is called the 'Phoolwalon ki sair' or more formally in Persian—'Sair-e-Gulfaroshan'. Floral offerings are made at the shrine of Qutub Sahib and also at the temple of the goddess Jog Maya, which is near Adham Khan's tomb.

The entrance to Zafar Mahal is through a **large doorway (6)**, said to have been constructed by Bahadur Shah to allow elephants to enter. The inscription on the marble slab over the doorway gives the date 1264 Hijri or 1847–48. On either side of the doorway, note the jharokhas with curved 'bangla' roofs, very much a late Mughal feature.

Once inside, the passageway leading straight from the doorway has some interesting painted ornamentation. In style some of this looks quite European, and we know that a couple of Bahadur Shah's brothers were quite interested in Western architecture. The rooms beyond are in a rather ruined condition. Another passage goes off to the left of the entrance and this will take you into an open space with more or less ruined rooms ranged around.

A series of rooms on your left here have lost their roofs, which were presumably made of wood and have perished. You can see what was a **double-storeyed section (7)** has some interesting features. It has a border running along the top of the roof which has painting and a balustrade of a distinctly European style. One of the rooms on the upper floor has a Western-style fireplace.

An opening in the wall across from this building takes you into a courtyard that is very distinctly in the traditional late Mughal style. Note the cusped or scalloped arches placed on delicate pillars. In the north-eastern part of this courtyard is a **grave enclosure (8)** made of marble lattice screens. This houses three Mughal graves. The most central one is that of the Mughal emperor Bahadur Shah I (reigned 1707–12). Immediately to the west of it lies the grave of the emperor Shah Alam II (reigned 1759–1806). To the west of Shah Alam II's grave is that of Akbar II, who was the father of Bahadur Shah Zafar and the son of Shah Alam II. To the east of the grave of Bahadur Shah I is the grave of Mirza Fakhru, son of Zafar.

Between the graves of Bahadur Shah I and that of Shah Alam II is an empty place which is frequently pointed out

as the space left vacant for the emperor Bahadur Shah Zafar. Zafar was the last Mughal emperor, who was exiled to Rangoon, Burma, for his part in the uprising against British rule in 1857, and he died there some years later. This is actually a curious backward projection because the place could not have been 'left vacant' in the time of either Bahadur Shah I or even Shah Alam II. The floor of the enclosure was always paved, and part of it was dug up for each subsequent burial. It is not conceivable that the floor was dug up in preparation for Zafar's body when it was clearly not there.

There are some other graves outside the enclosure, which belong to other, less important members of the Mughal royal family.

A doorway set in the wall immediately to the east of the grave enclosure leads to a small white marble mosque, known as the **Moti Masjid (9)** or 'pearl mosque'. Built by the emperor Bahadur Shah I in 1809, it is reasonably attractive, though not breathtaking. On the western side is the covered portion of the mosque with the qibla wall. Notice that on the eastern side of this mosque, across the high wall, you can see the dome of the shrine of Qutub Sahib. Probably the mosque was originally much more integrated with the shrine. In 1857, after Bahadur Shah was exiled, the royal properties were appropriated by the British government. It is likely that the strict division between the shrine and this complex dates from that time.

Return to the courtyard with the grave enclosure. Through the dalan on the west, you can see some structures that are

Kitna hai badnaseeb Zafar Dafan ke liye Do gaz zameen bhi Mil na saki ku e yaar mein (How luckless is Zafar, that he could not get two yards of land to be buried in his beloved's lane - A curiously prophetic couplet by Zafar)

10

very different in style—heavily built stone pavilions. Note the solid grey quartzite columns and the heavy striped dome. These are the **oldest part of the complex (10)**. It is said that a nephew of the emperor Iltutmish, and a disciple of Qutub Sahab are buried in the square pavilion tomb just north of the domed pavilion. Clearly, the Mughal palace was built around these older structures.

To the north of these is a broad staircase that leads to a higher level, in fact to rooms built over the grand gateway of Zafar through which you first entered. This kind of staircase also betrays a European influence. In Indian architecture, staircases were seen as necessary but ugly things that broke up a nice façade. They were therefore to be made as inconspicuous as possible, preferably hidden in the thick-

ness of a wall. In most traditional Indian buildings you will find that the staircases are steep and narrow, often entered through low doorways. So this was a major innovation.

Climb up the stairs, and to the right you will come across more stairs (this time more like the ones you expect in an old Indian building). These will lead you to the top of the gateway. This is essentially an open pillared verandah overlooking the main street at the foot of the palace. The pillars are slender late-Mughal ones. There is one interesting detail. The pillars in the outer row, facing the street, are made of marble. The pillars to the inside are simply covered with limestone plaster. The resources of the last emperor were straitened but he still wanted to make a show. So the pillars that were in view of the public were marble, but those farther in could get away with mimicking it!

Leave Zafar Mahal the way you came and take the lane on your left from in front of the gate. It is a short lane and on it you will see two rectangular **Mughal tombs (11)**, probably from the sixteenth century. They are now in use, one as a home and one as a shop.

The lane soon intersects with a broad and busy street which is the main bazaar of Mehrauli village. This was once the main road to Gurgaon and in fact till the mid-nineteenth century it went past Zafar Mahal. It was Bahadur Shah Zafar who arranged to have it realigned so it would not pass directly under the gate of his palace. This had been a cause for inconvenience to passers-by, who had to respectfully dismount every time they went past the gate.

Turn left into this road. It is very busy but particularly if you are there at a quiet time of day you might be able to concentrate on some interesting architecture along the way.

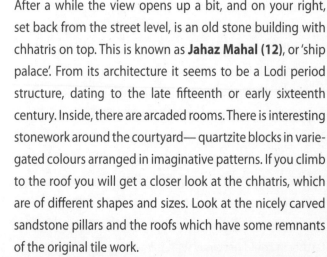

After a while the view opens up a bit, and on your right, set back from the street level, is an old stone building with chhatris on top. This is known as **Jahaz Mahal (12)**, or 'ship palace'. From its architecture it seems to be a Lodi period structure, dating to the late fifteenth or early sixteenth century. Inside, there are arcaded rooms. There is interesting stonework around the courtyard— quartzite blocks in variegated colours arranged in imaginative patterns. If you climb to the roof you will get a closer look at the chhatris, which are of different shapes and sizes. Look at the nicely carved sandstone pillars and the roofs which have some remnants of the original tile work.

From the roof you can also appreciate the location of the building as it is on the edge of a water body, hence the imagery of a 'ship' palace in the name. This tank is the **Hauz-e-Shamsi (13)**, and there is an interesting story attached to it. In the early days of the Delhi Sultanate the population of Mehrauli was growing and the emperor Iltutmish wanted to build a water reservoir for the city. It is said that one day the Prophet Mohammad appeared to him in a dream, riding a horse, and told the ruler to build the tank at the spot he had appeared in. The next morning Iltutmish went with Qutub Sahab to inspect the area and found the spot, with the mark of a horse's hoof on it. The tank was dug in that location, around the year 1229–30.

The reservoir was an ambitious enterprise, occupying a large area, and being fed by underground springs as well as streams. The **pavilion (14)** you see across the tank from the Jahaz Mahal once stood in the middle of the water. It covered a stone slab with the mark of a hoof print, believed to have been made by the horse the Prophet was riding. The tank had a tendency to get silted up and required repeated excavation—first by Alauddin Khalji and then Firoz Shah Tughlaq. According to some sources, it was the former who had the pavilion built, but the building now standing there is distinctly of the Lodi period in its style.

On the same side of the road as Jahaz Mahal, a little further down, is an easy-to-miss modern mosque. The current building is however located at the site of one of the first mosques to be built in India—the **Auliya Masjid (15)**, or 'saints' mosque'. This is believed to be a spot where the

saints, Muinuddin Chishti and Qutubuddin Bakhtiyar Kaki, offered prayers, and the original mosque is said to have been built by Iltutmish.

16

On the other side of the bazaar road from Jahaz Mahal, and down a slope is the last destination on this walk—**Jharna (16)** or a 'waterfall', now dry. It was an overflow from the reservoir during the rainy season which was diverted to this spot by way of an attractive cascade. This waterfall was developed as a recreational area around the year 1700, by an important Mughal nobleman of the time of Aurangzeb, Nawab Ghaziuddin Khan. Ghaziuddin Khan incidentally was the father of Nizam-ul-Mulk, prime minister of the Mughal Empire and founder of the independent state of Hyderabad.

Ghaziuddin Khan built the small pavilion through which the water flowed into the garden, and the tank in front of

it. In time other structures were added to the garden. Akbar II added the pavilion to the north, and Bahadur Shah Zafar added the pavilion in the middle. The later Mughals used to come to this place to picnic on a regular basis in the rainy season, and it became one of the venues for the Phoolwalon ki Sair. This is in fact still the case.

MEHRAULI
ARCHAEOLOGICAL PARK

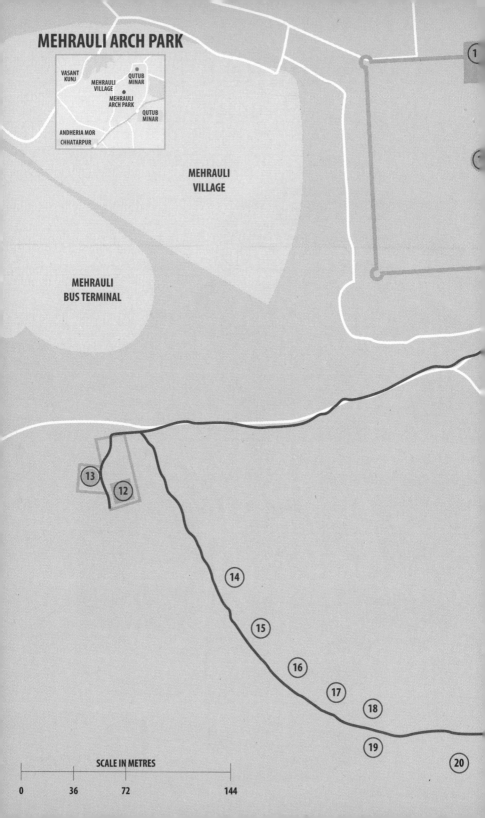

MEHRAULI ARCH PARK

VASANT
KUNJ

MEHRAULI
VILLAGE

QUTUB
MINAR

MEHRAULI
ARCH PARK

QUTUB
MINAR

ANDHERIA MOR
CHHATARPUR

MEHRAULI
VILLAGE

MEHRAULI
BUS TERMINAL

SCALE IN METRES

0   36   72   144

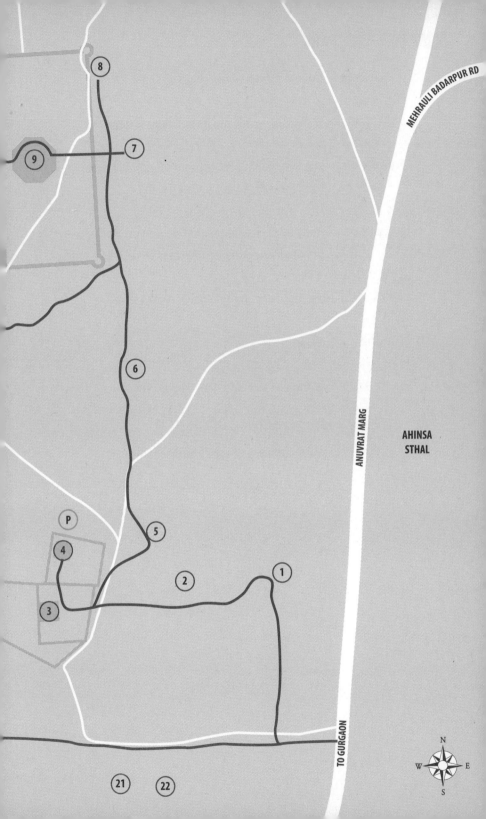

Timings:	Open during daylight hours all week.
Tickets:	Entry to the park and its buildings is free.
Highlights:	Maulana Jamali's mosque and tomb, Dilkusha, Rajon ki baoli (best for an abbreviated walk).
Difficulty Level:	Fairly even pleasant paths through the park. Steep steps have to be negotiated to access Dilkusha.
Metro Station:	Qutub Minar on the Yellow line, 0.5 km.
Amenities:	None.
Parking:	At the site, near Maulana Jamali's mosque.
Tip:	Locally this area is called 'Jamali-Kamali' and few people will recognize the park's formal name.

SYLVAN RETREAT

Mehrauli is probably the oldest continuously inhabited area of Delhi, and the archaeological park lies adjacent to it. It has some fascinating buildings set in pleasant parkland, some of it landscaped. This park lies alongside the southern edges of the now barely discernable fort walls of Lal Kot. When Lal Kot was the fortified centre of the capital city of the Delhi Sultanate, some buildings, such as the tomb of the emperor Balban had begun to be located just outside the southern walls. Slowly the population grew in this area and habitation spread along the valley which sloped down from the higher ground on which Lal Kot was situated. The population flourished even after the capital shifted away from Mehrauli in the fourteenth century. More buildings came up here—mosques, tombs, baolis, gardens and houses.

In the nineteenth century, when the British administered Delhi, Mehrauli was a popular location for second 'country homes'. The British as well as the prosperous local residents of Delhi, which was then in Shahjahanabad, now called 'old Delhi', spent some time here as it was believed to have a healthier air than the city.

A considerable stream drained this area, collecting water from the catchment areas on the ridge on which Mehrauli is located. Over the centuries this stream also carried down silt into the valley, covering up lower layers of construction. In fact many of the structures of the archaeological park have been fully unearthed only quite recently, some still lie half-buried.

THE WALK

A convenient place to begin the walk is **Balban's Tomb (1)** which lies close to the main gate into the park, located on the Mehrauli Gurgaon road. Just within the gate, turn right and walk up the path to a ruined stone entrance way. This has some distinctive features of early Sultanate architecture. It is made of the locally available, hard, quartzite stone. The doorway is corbelled, a construction technique that was prevalent before the Turks brought a knowledge of the arch to India. The dome is a curious pyramidal-shape, which has happened because arch-making principles have not been used in its construction.

The gateway leads into a paved courtyard, which until quite recently was covered over with earth and vegetation. At the

other end lies a large square building, which is the tomb of the emperor Balban. He was originally the slave of the emperor Iltutmish, and after the failed reigns of several of the latter's children, Balban became Sultan, or ruler. He ruled from 1266–87.

The building appears quite plain and its basic construction material is exposed. Some remains of red sandstone on the outside, particularly the doorway that is across from the main entrance, however suggest that it might have been used as an ornamental facing. There is no cenotaph in the room, probably because it might have been made of a valuable stone that was stolen. In an adjoining room however there is a large cenotaph covered with red sandstone. This is believed to mark the grave of the son of Balban, who was given the title 'Khan Shahid' or 'martyr prince', after he died in battle with the Mongols during Balban's lifetime.

From beside this tomb chamber a small flight of stone steps leads to an area at a higher level, which is covered by ruins. All that survives are walls, mostly low, which are the remains of a dense **residential settlement (2)**, dating to the Mughal period. Walk through this area in the direction leading away from Balban's tomb, and you will soon come to substantial gateposts, which are nineteenth century British additions to the area. Opposite these, across the narrow motorable track lies the **mosque of Maulana Jamali (3)**.

The courtyard you enter is a quiet, shady place with a pool that is now empty but would have originally contained water for wuzu. The person who commissioned this mosque was a Sufi saint and poet called Shaikh Fazlullah, alias Jalal Khan, who is better known by his takhallus or pen name of Jamali. He lived under the Lodi and Mughal dynasties and was equally respected by emperors of both. The mosque, built in 1528, is of a style that reflects the transition between Lodi and Mughal architecture. The western side, as in all mosques denotes the direction of prayer or qibla. Note that

4

the arched doorway is set in the large central arch. Above this, is a small, arched opening, with a base supported on carved, stone brackets—an architectural feature that is very typical of this period. On either side of the large, middle arch there are red sandstone pilasters, which mimic the Qutub Minar, in style. Inside the covered part of the mosque, the western wall has the mihrabs which indicate the direction of prayer.

From within the courtyard of the mosque an opening to the north, (you can orient yourself if you remember which is the western side of the mosque), leads you into an enclosure within which stands the **tomb of Maulana Jamali (4)**. He died in 1536 in Gujarat where he had gone with the emperor Humayun, who was engaged in the conquest of that province. It is said that Maulana Jamali's body was brought back

to Delhi and he was buried 'in the room in which he had lived'. If so, the heavily ornamented room within which his grave is located makes fairly improbable living quarters.

Nevertheless, it is an exquisite piece of work and easily the star attraction of the park. The inside is covered with an intricately incised and painted plaster, combined with brilliantly coloured tiles. Along the top of the walls there are panels inscribed with the Persian verses of Maulana Jamali. The western side of the room has a marble mihrab, at the base of which, is the pattern of a kalash with mango leaves in the mouth. The combination of these symbols powerfully supports the theory of religious and cultural syncretism and tolerance represented by the Sufi saints.

The grave in the centre of the room is that of Jamali. To the east of that is the grave of an unknown person. Like the grave of Maulana Jamali, this too has the qalamdan which signifies that it is the grave of a man. This was obviously a close associate of the saint, to have been entitled to a spot in the same room. We do not know who he was but popular lore has given him the name 'Kamali', probably just to rhyme with Jamali rather than for any historical reasons. The mosque, tomb and often the whole surrounding area

'By one shower from the cloud of beneficence you wash away the dust of crime from our ashamed face.

Cast your eyes upon Jamali with kindness and do not look at his idleness and shortcoming.'
(Two couplets by Jamali, inscribed within the tomb.)

is popularly known as 'Jamali-Kamali'. Outside, in the court-yard and in another enclosure to the east of it, there are many other graves. One of them is under a chhatri, and is clearly the grave of a woman because it has a takhti made on it.

Go back through the mosque and when you leave the courtyard, turn left. The area before you is landscaped and covered with grass. On a high grassy mound on the right is a **domed, stone canopy (5)**. Though it looks older, it was actually built in the 1840s by Thomas Metcalfe, who was the highest British administrative official in Delhi. It is in the tradition of British 'follies' of that period—structures that were meant to look old or exotic and add picturesque appeal to the landscape.

5

Continue along the path for just a bit and then go straight up the next rise in the ground, which has a **well (6)** on top. On the other side, the ground slopes away again and you will see a broad carriageway, with a low parapet wall on either side. Go up the carriage way and it will bring you to a shady clearing surrounded by buildings. This area formed part of Thomas Metcalfe's estate in Mehrauli where he built or modified several buildings to make for himself, a comfortable and beautiful retreat from the city, which at that time was in Shahjahanabad to the north.

To your right will be an amorphous structure known as the **Kabutar Khana (7)** or 'pigeon house' **or boathouse**. This was a Mughal building that was modified by Metcalfe to form a landing stage for boats. On the other side is the depression in the ground, now covered with vegetation, which was filled with water to create a lake. On the roof of the building there are small niches, which would have held the pigeons that were also kept here, one assumes for recreation.

Going back into the clearing, turn right to go into a **circular building (8)**. This was constructed from scratch in the time of Metcalfe and seems to have been a sitting or dining room. The circular inner room has a small decorative fireplace, and spacious shelves. The outer gallery has ledges that might have facilitated the service of food. The roof, of which nothing remains, was probably supported on wooden beams as the slots where they would have fitted can still be seen.

9

Returning to the clearing, turn right and go up the broad flight of steps which will eventually bring you to the building which is **Quli Khan's tomb (9)** but also known as **Dilkusha**. Quli Khan was the son of Maham Angah, the emperor Akbar's wet nurse. He died in the early seventeenth century and was buried on this spot not far from the Qutub Minar. The octagonal tomb has some beautifully painted and incised plaster decoration that has recently been restored to its original brilliance. There is no cenotaph marking the place of burial. It has obviously disappeared, though the body was buried in the ground, far below. On one side of the building there are the remains of some attached walls, in a style very different from that of the tomb. This is a clue to what happened to the building in the mid-nineteenth century. Thomas Metcalfe converted it into a house by adding rooms on all sides, and named it Dilkusha which means 'delightful'. He surrounded it with a garden, land-

scaped with terraces, pavilions and watercourses. The family of Metcalfe appears not to have used the building after the revolt of 1857. Probably at some later date, the archaeology department dismantled most of Metcalfe's additions, leaving just a portion by way of a sample.

In the grounds behind Dilkusha is another of **Metcalfe's canopies (10)**. Painted in red, on the ceiling, is a circular pattern of fishes. Not far, in the direction of the Qutub Minar, which at this point dominates the skyline, is another building modified by Metcalfe. This is likely to have been a Mughal period gateway that connected the Qutub Minar precincts with the grounds of Quli Khan's tomb. Metcalfe added rooms to it to create an **annexe (11)** to the main house. The first section that you enter has a row of curious, somewhat narrow, pointed arches. The next wall has circular arches. These walls were added in the nineteenth century. The inner room also has a fireplace. Beyond that is the original Mughal gate, with a broad, pointed arch. Its Mughal character is also evident in the net vaulting pattern in the area where the arch meets the wall. Another British addition is the small plunge pool constructed behind this wall. If you look carefully to the left, you can see the opening from where the water once entered the pool. On the other side of the wall, (not visible from here) is the well which supplied the water.

Steps lead to the roof of this building. It is worth climbing up, for the breathtaking view it gives of the Qutub Minar. It is quite clear why Thomas Metcalfe picked this spot!

Go back to the tomb and down the flight of steps. On the way back to Quli Khan's tomb, look for signs of the old water channels that were a decorative element of the garden. Proceed back along the carriageway and at the end of it, turn right, to join a path that proceeds further along in the same direction. A moderate walk of a few minutes will bring you to some ruins clustered among trees. These are mainly tombs and grave platforms from the fifteenth century.

12

On the left of the path there is a more significant group of buildings, the **Rajon ki Bain/Baoli (12)** and an adjacent mosque and tomb. The baoli dates from the Lodi period

and is a large one. The steps would have given access to the water, which would be spread out in a pool at the bottom. There is also a more conventional well opening at the far end. People would have come here from the neighbouring settlement, maybe with bundles of clothes or dishes to wash. Once the clothes had been washed (probably away from the pool itself) and left out to dry, one could relax for a few hours in the shade of the rooms surrounding the well. The name 'raj' means 'mason', thus 'baoli of masons'. Maybe this name was given because at some time the baoli was used by a group of masons.

A doorway and some steps take you to a higher level where there is a **tomb and a mosque (13)**. The tomb, which is in the form of a chhatri or pavillion over a grave, has an inscription on the southern side. The language is somewhat

13

ambiguous but it tells us that this building was constructed in 1506 during the reign of Sikandar Lodi by Daulat Khan, possibly over the remains of Khwaja Mohammad. It is likely that this tomb was constructed about the same time as the baoli, in which case we have a date for the latter. On the ceiling of the chhatri there is a

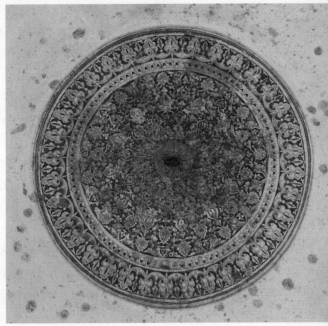

circular pattern made of red paint, which suggests that this was the inspiration for Metcalfe's canopy ceiling.

Close to the tomb is a mosque, presumably built at the same time. It is fairly small but has the fine incised plaster that is characteristic of the Lodi period. It appears that the mosque was occupied as a home for quite some time as the plaster inside is blackened with soot. A decorative doorway leads from the platform on which the mosque and chhatri are located, down some steps to the other side of the baoli. By following this somewhat overgrown route, you can get a view of the back of the well, which has quite a nice, round shape and is decorated with plaster.

Through the scrub at this point you will be able to see some buildings fairly close by. One is a wall mosque, now white-washed and in use. Closer in there is an enclosure which might have been a sarai (a medieval inn) or a residence. Beside this is a path that leads in a south-easterly direction back through the park. If the area behind the baoli is very overgrown you might like to go back the way you entered the baoli complex, and join this path from the other side.

Beside the path, shortly you will see a large sunken area containing a group of buildings from different periods. The largest, by architectural style datable to the Mughal period, consists of a **pillared hall (14)** at one end of an enclosure. The path goes over a bridge and parallel to what was the old channel of the major stream that once drained the area. Now it is a noxious drain, mainly directed through a large underground pipe. As you go along you will see various

buildings beside the path. On the left are two identical box-like structures, probably **gatehouses (15)** from the Metcalfe era. A little further on, also on your left you will see a **building with jharokhas (16)**, half-buried, its jharokhas almost at ground level. This indicates the extent to which the silt brought down by the stream covered up the buildings beside it. The style and positioning of the jharokhas suggests that this building might have been a fifteenth century gateway.

Next to this building is a **tomb (17)** located right behind a **wall mosque**, both probably from the early Mughal period. Beyond this is a long arcaded building believed to be Mughal era **stables (18)**. On the other side of the path is a compound that contains the **mosque of Maulana Majduddin (19)** with an attached graveyard. This is now in use and has been whitewashed.

Proceeding a little further down the path, on the right there is a barred stone gateway leading into a garden, now in private ownership and out of bounds for the public. This is the **Bagh-e-Nazir (20)**, a large garden laid out in 1748 by Roz Afzun Nazir the Khwajasara or chief eunuch of the Mughal emperor Mohammad Shah.

Next, again to your right, is a slightly raised **walled enclosure (21)**. This is evidently a tomb set within a garden. You can particularly see the remains of water features. The tomb building is very ruined though you can see some remaining walls with pretty plasterwork. The ornamentation clearly indicates that it is of the Mughal period. Adjacent to this

22

enclosure and entered through it, is a space that contains an attractive rectangular **pavilion (22)**. A local tradition developed here at some point which held that this was the tomb of Khan Shahid, the son of Balban. This is clearly highly improbable, firstly because Khan Shahid is believed to be buried in the chamber next to his father's. Secondly, the style of this building, with its shallow relief incised plasterwork, is quite certainly Mughal. The ceiling is particularly beautiful, with Quranic verses inscribed in an unusual pattern.

This brings you nearly to the gate of the archaeological park, and the end of the walk.

KASHMIRI GATE

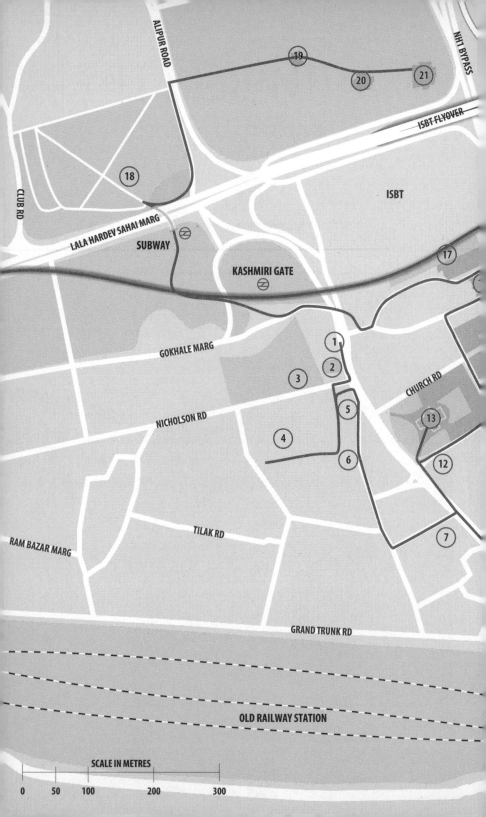

ALIPUR ROAD

NH1 BYPASS

⑲

⑳

㉑

ISBT FLYOVER

CLUB RD

⑱

ISBT

LALA HARDEV SAHAI MARG

SUBWAY

KASHMIRI GATE

⑰

GOKHALE MARG

①

②

③

CHURCH RD

⑤

⑬

NICHOLSON RD

④

⑥

⑫

RAM BAZAR MARG

TILAK RD

⑦

GRAND TRUNK RD

OLD RAILWAY STATION

SCALE IN METRES

0   50   100   200   300

KASHMIRI GATE

TIS HAZARI

KASHMIRI GATE

OLD DELHI RLY STN

SALIMGARH FORT

CHANDNI CHOWK

(11)

KELA GHAT MARG

MAHATMA GANDHI MARG

(9)

(8)

(10)

LOTHIAN RD

MA PRASAD MUKHERJI MARG

N

W E

S

Timings: Such buildings as you can enter are open through the day all week, except the Museum of Archaeology which you cannot go inside on Saturdays and Sundays.

Tickets: Free.

Highlights: St James' Church, Nicholson Cemetery, Qudsia Bagh, Dara Shikoh Library.

Difficulty Level: The walk is mostly on the pavements along busy roads. Watch out for traffic.

Metro Station: Kashmiri Gate on the Yellow line, 0.15 km.

Amenities: None in particular.

Parking: Official parking lot next to the Metro station, or on the street next to St James' Church.

NORTHERN SHAHJAHANABAD

The area covered in this walk is the north-eastern corner of the city of Shahjahanabad, built by the Mughal emperor Shahjahan in the mid-seventeenth century as a planned imperial capital. Kashmiri Gate, so named because it faced the north, towards Kashmir, was one of the gates in the city wall. This was a part of the city that was right next to the Red Fort or the palace complex where the emperor himself lived. At the same time it also overlooked the river Yamuna. These factors made it prime real estate, and it was there-fore the site of the mansions of some very important people. Shahjahan's favourite son Dara Shikoh had his estate here, as did the nobleman Ali Mardan Khan.

In the eighteenth century there was a decline in the fortunes of some of these grandees and a decline of the Mughal Empire itself. The estates fell into disrepair, but for some reason did not get built up as was the case with many other areas of the city. In the early nineteenth century there was a revival. The British East India Company was the new power in the region, with an administration in Delhi on a reasonably significant scale. This establishment came to be housed in the area around Kashmiri Gate, still a relatively sought-after prime property. Some of the old buildings were taken over and transformed into 'colonial' buildings by the clever addition of façades. Others were built from scratch.

Soon, apart from houses and offices, this area had a church, a cemetery, a college, and a powder magazine where ammunition was manufactured and stored. Then came the uprising of 1857 and Delhi was a major centre. From May to September, the city ran an independent administration

and by the time it was recaptured by the British some things had changed—the magazine buildings had been blown up and the gate itself was badly damaged. A new cemetery had to be built just outside the gate to accommodate those who died in the fighting.

Soon after the railway line was driven through the centre of the city, cutting the Kashmiri Gate area off from the rest of Shahjahanabad. It still continued to be a fashionable place to live—until New Delhi overtook it by the middle of the twentieth century. Kashmiri Gate today is quieter and less crowded than other parts of Shahjahanabad like Chandni Chowk, and there is a lot to see.

THE WALK

Kashmiri Gate (1) is one of the thirteen original gates of the city of Shahjanahanabad. It is unusually placed in relation to the city wall. If you look at the line of the wall that stretches on either side, the gate is placed at a sharp angle in the wall. It is mainly built of the thin strong bricks characteristic of Mughal architecture, with some use

of sandstone. The severe damage that is still evident was caused by the storming of this gate which allowed the British forces to enter the city on 14 September 1857.

Leave the gate and walk on to the pavement on the right. You will first pass the **Bengali Club (2)**. Bengalis were an important component of the British administrative staff, and their numbers increased with the shift of the capital of the British Empire from Calcutta to Delhi in 1912. Many of them lived around Kashmiri Gate, and with them came their social and cultural institutions. The Kashmiri Gate Durga puja, the oldest community Durga puja festival in Delhi, began here in 1910, and is still an annual event. The Bengali club building was constructed in 1925.

If you turn into the street right after the club you can walk along the **city wall (3)**. To your left lies the area that was a popular residential area till the mid-twentieth century. It

4

still has some old colonial buildings. Turn into the first arched gateway to the left and walk to the end of that short street. Turn right and a short way down you will see

on your right the red-painted **Sultan Singh building (4)**, which was built in the 1890s by Lala Sultan Singh, a rich industrialist of Delhi. It is of an exuberantly eclectic style, combining several Western and Indian elements.

Turn back from here and take the street going straight. It curves to the left and presently you will come to a narrow lane leading off it to the right. Take this and it will bring you to a building just south of the Bengali club. This is the **Kashmiri Gate Market (5)** building, constructed in the 1890s by Sultan Singh. Note the wrought iron pillars and ornamentation.

6

Walk southwards from here and on the same side of the street you will come to the **Fakhr-ul-Masjid (6)** or the 'pride of mosques'. The main body of the mosque is on the upper floor. This was a common arrangement, as the lower floor was usually occupied by shops, the rent from which was allocated for the upkeep of the mosque. You can enter the mosque. An inscription over the central arch tells us that this mosque was built in the year 1728–29 by a lady called Kaniz Fatima, in memory of her husband Shujat Khan, a nobleman. The bulbous striped domes and the minarets

topped by lanterns are typical of the late Mughal architectural style.

In the early nineteenth century this mosque as well as a large tract of land behind and on both sides of it belonged to Colonel James Skinner, one of the colourful characters of early colonial Delhi. He was the son of an English father and an Indian mother, and began his career as a mercenary soldier under the Marathas. During the Anglo-Maratha wars he came over to the British side with the troops under his command. The troops under him formed an 'irregular' regiment as it was not formally a part of the British Indian army, known as Skinner's Horse, which is in fact still a part of the Indian army.

For James Skinner, crossing over from the Maratha side to the British also ultimately led to a conscious desire to emphasize the British side of his ancestry. He sent his sons to England to be educated. He sold his house in Chandni Chowk and instead bought a large estate in the Kashmiri Gate area where the British used to live. Fakhr-ul-Masjid was on his estate, and Skinner had the mosque repaired so his retainers could use it. The popular story that he had vowed to build a mosque and a church when lying injured on a battlefield, is unverified.

After the mosque, turn into the broad street to the left, and on your right you will see a large grey stone building. This now houses the offices of the Election Commission, but was built in 1890 for **St Stephen's College (7)**. St Stephen's College, which began functioning in 1881 out of a modest town house or haveli in Chandni Chowk, soon shifted to this imposing building, more in keeping with its status as the premier Western style institution of its time. The building is an eclectic mix of Mughal and Western features and styles. The former include chhatris, the chhajja, and the patterned border over it. Western influences are evident in the square porch and balustrade over it. The architect was Swinton Jacob, a proponent of the 'Indo-Saracenic' style of architecture which sought to incorporate features of Indian 'Islamic' architecture into Classical and Gothic revivalist styles.

Turn right on the main road in front of St Stephen's College building and somewhat further down and soon you should see, in an island in the middle of the road, what remains of the **Magazine (8)**. The magazine was a large compound with several buildings, where ammunition was manufactured and stored for the British army. In 1857, when Indian rebel troops took over the city, the British officials in charge of the magazine decided to blow it up rather than allow it to fall into rebel hands, and that is what they did. Only these gateposts remain.

To the north of the gates is a granite column put up in 1901 to honour personnel from the postal department who died in the uprising of 1857. Cross over to the other side of the road now and you will see a nice looking **General Post Office (9)** building dating from 1885. This was obviously built on the site of the old magazine.

A little further down the road, to the left is one of the oldest Christian cemeteries in Delhi—**Lothian Cemetery (10)**, established in 1808. It is in a pitiable condition, as for many years it was encroached upon by people who had built their homes here. Here and there you may still see some interesting tombstones and plaques.

Turn back from this point and travel northwards on the same side of the road. You will come to a gate on the right that leads into the campus of the Guru Gobind Singh Indraprastha University. Enter this and if asked, say that you want to go to the Delhi Department of Archaeology Museum in the Dara Shikoh Library. The building known as

the **Dara Shikoh Library (11)** on the outside has a rather plain neoclassical façade, but it is a delightfully complex structure. This is because it was actually a converted Mughal mansion. This building was part of the estate of Dara Shikoh, the scholarly son of Shahjahan, until that prince was killed on orders of his brother Aurangzeb in 1659. For sometime in the eighteenth century the mansion was in the possession of a Portuguese lady called Juliana, and then it was sold to Safdarjang, the prime minister.

In the early nineteenth century it was bought by David Ochterlony, the first British 'Resident' in Delhi after the British East India Company took over the administration in 1803. The title of Resident harked back to the time when the Resident was simply a sort of ambassador to the court of the Mughal emperor. After 1803 the Resident was the head of the British administration in Delhi as well as a mediator of British relations with the several neighbouring independent and semi-independent states in the region. Ochterlony bought this building to serve as an office, and when Ochterlony left it was bought by the British government as a permanent 'Residency' for the Resident.

Considerable pains and expense were taken to turn the Mughal mansion into a suitably British-looking structure. A façade of Ionic columns was tagged on, and the original façade of Mughal arches was covered over with solid masonry. If you go inside you can see some of the original features that have been revealed in recent years. If you go around to the back of the building you can see a lower floor of red sandstone arches, and ornamental baluster columns inside, which are part of the original structure. On the side of the building, set high in the wall, is a simple plaque— 'Once the Residency'.

In 1844 for various reasons the Residency was moved to Ludlow Castle, a building outside Kashmiri Gate; and the Delhi College was moved into this building. The Delhi College was the first European-style college in Delhi, where Western sciences were taught through the medium of the Urdu language. Prominent alumni included the Mathematician Master Ramchander and educationist Zakaullah. During the uprising of 1857 the college was attacked and its library and laboratory were destroyed. Later in the century a school was housed in this building, and in a new block which was built to the south east of it.

Return to the gate of the university campus and carry on further northwards on the same pavement. To your right, across from the St Stephen's College building, you can see a block of buildings similar in style to the college. These were the St Stephen's College **hostel buildings (12)**.

12

After you pass the St Stephen's College buildings, you will see **St James' Church (13)** on your right. This church was built in 1835 by Colonel James Skinner, whom we met earlier. Skinner had been raised as a Muslim and converted to Christianity rather late in life. He wished to move in local British social circles, and the building of the church helped to establish him within the local British community. He was baptized in the church with his sons when it was consecrated in 1836.

13

The neoclassical church building has the dome positioned in the centre— an unusual shape for a church. In the garden in front of the building there is a memorial in the shape of a large cross, to those Christians who were killed in the uprising of 1857. Next to that is a sandstone platform that once had a beautiful marble memorial on it. It was a memorial to William Fraser, a British official who eventually rose to be Resident. Fraser was a somewhat controversial figure who had made himself unpopular in some quarters. One night in 1835 he was murdered on his way back home. The crime was traced back to Nawab Shamsuddin Khan, an important nobleman of Delhi. Shamsuddin was charged with having engaged an assassin to kill Fraser, he was held guilty and hanged. The trial was controversial as many of the citizens of Delhi protested that it had not been conducted fairly. The circumstances of his death and its aftermath made Fraser disliked even in death. Fraser was a close friend of James Skinner, who had a memorial constructed in a prominent place within the yard of the church, which was then under construction. When the uprising broke out in 1857, this tomb was savagely attacked and broken up. Interestingly, other graves in the churchyard were unharmed. You can walk around and see some of these.

On one side of the church an enclosure surrounded by an iron railing contains graves of the Skinner family. Look at the inscriptions in Persian, which was the lingua franca in north India till well into the nineteenth century, when English replaced it as the language of higher learning and communication, and of the upper rungs of the administration and law courts. At the back of the church there is also the grave of Thomas Metcalfe, who was Resident and Commissioner of Delhi for many years before his death in 1853.

Skinner died in 1841 and is buried within the church itself, so this is a good time to see the inside of the building. Look at the beautiful stained glass inside the church. This was restored early in the twenty-first century. As you approach the altar there are two panels in the floor. The first has a colourful pattern of a tree and is a fragment from the tomb of William Fraser. Between this and the altar is the stone under which Skinner is buried.

Look at the many plaques within the church. They give details about worshippers in this church down the years. Notice the long relationship between the church, the Skinner family and the Skinner's Horse regiment.

As you leave the church gate, turn left and then left again. This will bring you in front of the St Stephen's hostel buildings. Walk along the church compound wall and at the end turn left and continue to walk behind the church. When you reach the corner where the church land comes to an end, look right and you should see a building belonging to the  **Northern Railways (14)**. This is another Mughal mansion that was transformed into an English building— and a rather ornate one! Look at the fussy turrets and arches. Unfortunately it is not normally possible to go inside the building. It has a capacious taikhana or a series of underground chambers which were much cooler than ground-level rooms and so were used as living rooms in the summer. It seems that this building was used as a home by the Resident while he carried out official business in the Residency.

Beyond the railways' building is another old government building, now occupied by the office of the **National Cadet Corp (15)**. It is an unpretentious structure, on the site where the British administration's criminal court was originally located. And behind it lies a curiosity, the **Gallows Bastion (16)**. When you walk around to the area behind the building you will be on top of the city wall. You will see a well-like hole in the ground. This is where the bodies of those who were hanged were lowered, so that their relations could pick them up from the area outside and below the wall.

Beyond this compound is a row of buildings that make up the **Old Court (17)**. The main court house was situated here during the early part of British rule. Now it is a Sub-registrar's office or a court at a fairly basic administrative level.

17

Walk back to Kashmiri Gate from here. On the other side of the metro station is a smallish patch of green known as Maharaja Agrasen Park. North of this park on the pavement is gate 3 of the Metro. This also serves as a subway pedestrian crossing to the other side of the road. Take it, and get out at gate 4. This will bring you up close to **Nicholson Cemetery (18)**.

18

Brigadier John Nicholson led the British forces that blew open Kashmiri Gate on 14 September 1857 to enter Delhi.

He was severely wounded and died a few days later. He became a popular hero to the British, and the new cemetery where he was buried was named after him. His grave lies near the entrance, surrounded by a railing. There are many other graves here, from 1857 and after. Read the inscriptions which incidentally reveal the low life expectancy of those times.

One of the graves here, on your right as you walk up the main path, is that of Master Ramchander—a mathematician who started his teaching career in the Delhi College. He was an original thinker who got some amount of international recognition. He was also very committed to the spread of scientific education in India. He ran a couple of newspapers which aimed at bringing scientific and other useful news to readers. He supported British rule and lived through the uprising of 1857, but was later very disillusioned with the racial discrimination faced by Indians.

If you walk along the road going north on the east of Nicholson Cemetery, across the road you will see a gate that leads into a garden. This is **Qudsia Bagh (19–21)**, or 'the garden of Qudsia'. Qudsia begam was a dancing girl who rose to be the wife of the Mughal emperor Mohammad Shah 'Rangila', who reigned from 1719–48. She became even more powerful when her son, Ahmad Shah, succeeded to the throne after her husband's death. It was then that she had this garden laid just outside the city walls.

The path that leads into the garden leads straight to a ruined **gateway (19)**. This is almost all that remains of a large, almost palace-like building, which is depicted in some old paintings. The buildings in this garden were severely damaged during the summer of 1857 when they fell in the line of fire that was exchanged between the Indian troops who were holding the fort, and the British troops who held the high ground on the ridge. The gateway displays some typical features of late Mughal architecture, such as the heavily applied stucco work decoration. There is some attractively carved red sandstone around the main arch too.

A little past the gateway, on the right is a **baradari (20)** or garden pavilion. It is located on the edge of a slope that led down to a substantial stream that fed into the Yamuna river. Now it is a drain with rather dirty water in it. The building is interesting because it was significantly modified, probably

in the late nineteenth century. Solid stone walls have been added to close up the arches and create additional rooms, and a sweeping staircase has been added in front. You can clearly make out the original features, which are executed in decorative stucco.

21

Further along the garden is the **mosque (21)**. Built at the same time as the garden, this too was badly damaged in 1857. You can see the huge craters that were gouged out when mortar hit the walls. The building is built of brick, covered in limestone plaster which has been decoratively carved and moulded.

CENTRAL VISTA

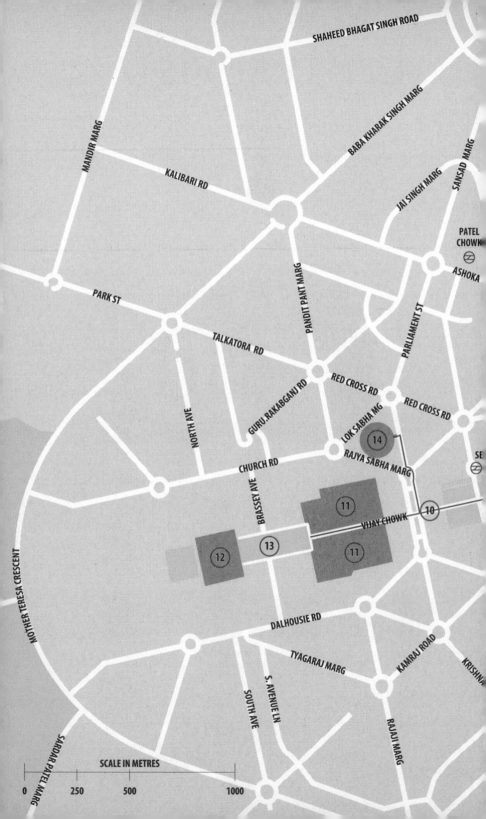

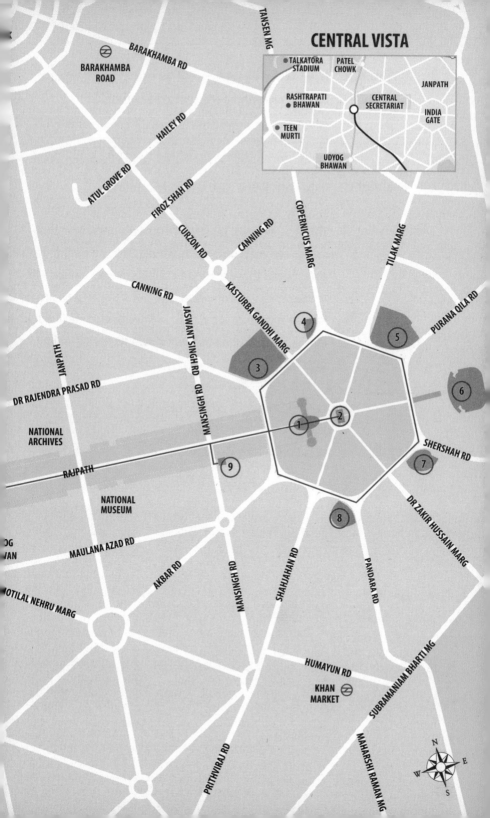

CENTRAL VISTA

- Talkatora Stadium
- Patel Chowk
- Janpath
- Rashtrapati Bhawan
- Central Secretariat
- India Gate
- Teen Murti
- Udyog Bhawan

TANSEN MG

BARAKHAMBA RD

BARAKHAMBA ROAD

HAILEY RD

ATUL GROVE RD

FIROZ SHAH RD

CURZON RD

CANNING RD

COPERNICUS MARG

TILAK MARG

CANNING RD

KASTURBA GANDHI MARG

PURANA QILA RD

JASWANT SINGH RD

④

⑤

③

JANPATH

⑥

DR RAJENDRA PRASAD RD

MANSINGH RD

NATIONAL ARCHIVES

①

②

SHERSHAH RD

RAJPATH

⑨

⑦

NATIONAL MUSEUM

⑧

DR ZAKIR HUSSAIN MARG

MAULANA AZAD RD

AKBAR RD

MANSINGH RD

SHAHJAHAN RD

PANDARA RD

OG WAN

MOTILAL NEHRU MARG

PRITHVIRAJ RD

HUMAYUN RD

KHAN MARKET

SUBRAMANIAM BHARTI MG

MAHARSHI RAMAN MG

N
W E
S

Timings: Open all day. Parliament, the Secretariat and Rashtrapati Bhawan can only be seen from the outside.

Tickets: Free.

Highlights: India Gate, Rashtrapati Bhawan, Secretariat.

Difficulty Level: This is a long walk, mostly on the pavements along busy roads. The walk route starts at India Gate, where there is parking, but those coming by public transport might like to start from the Metro station or bus stops at the Rajpath/ Rafi Marg intersection which is somewhere in the middle; in which case, just do the walk in two sections in either direction.

Metro Station: Central Secretariat on the Yellow line, 2 kms.

Amenities: Washrooms near Vijay Chowk.

Parking: At India Gate.

NEW DELHI

Over many centuries several cities had existed in the area we today know as Delhi. Incidentally there were more than 'seven cities of Delhi', a number that appears to have been arrived at out of a sense of romance rather than any factual basis. Each of them had occupied a distinct site, and gone by a distinct name—Indraprastha, Lal Kot/Qila Rai Pithora, Kilugarhi, Siri, Tughlaqabad, Jahanpanah, Firozabad, Mubarakabad, Dinpanah and Shahjahanabad.

The last episode in this saga took place in the second and third decades of the twentieth century, with the building of New Delhi. Since the decline of the Mughal Empire, Delhi had ceased to be a capital city in any real sense. From the early nineteenth century it was the British who controlled anything like an all-India empire, and their capital was at Calcutta. A turn in Delhi's fortunes came when the British monarch, George V, announced on 12 December 1911 that the capital of the empire was to be shifted to Delhi. The announcement was made in Delhi, which George V was visiting, to preside over the Coronation Darbar. This was a public spectacle designed to emphasize the position of the British Crown as the sovereign of the people of India, whether they lived

in territories directly administered by the British or in the numerous 'princely states' whose rulers were feudatories of the British Crown.

There were various political reasons for the decision to shift the capital away from Calcutta. The choice of Delhi as the alternative location was equally political. It was dictated largely by a desire to make a gesture that would, as the highest authorities in Britain and India believed, be popular through much of India. Popular belief associated the site of Delhi with Indraprastha of the Mahabharata; and for many

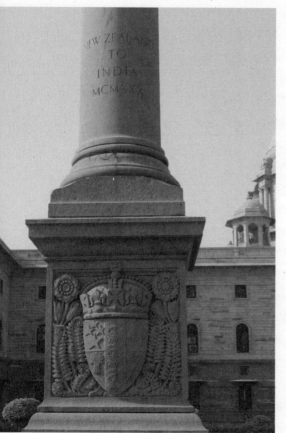

centuries, before the establishment of British rule, the capital of the empire had been in Delhi. The British government wanted to draw upon these symbolic associations to put forth their claim as legitimate successors to the great Indian empires.

An important part of this gesture of imperial authority was the decision to build a suitably impressive capital city. In fact the foundation stone was laid in the area where the Darbar was then in progress—north of Shahjahanabad. This was where the British administrative presence was then centred. This was also right next to the Ridge, which had sentimental value for the British for it was here that British forces had hung on in the months after the outbreak of the uprising in 1857, and from here they had launched their attack to retake the city.

The New Delhi Town Planning Committee decided that the site selected was not suitable. Instead, a site to the south of the seventeenth century Mughal city of Shahjahanabad was chosen. Plans were drawn up for an imperial city to be built on a grand scale. The British architect, Edwin Lutyens, was appointed to head the Town Planning Committee and to design the main public buildings. In view of the magnitude of the task, Herbert Baker was appointed as his associate.

There were many different influences that dictated the shape that the new city would take. Lutyens had a background, which included the design of the Hampstead Garden Suburb in London. From this came the conception of New Delhi as essentially a garden city, with residential houses set in large areas of green. There were also the examples of prominent capital cities around the world. The layout of Washington DC was a popular model, with the Capitol building at one end of a broad ceremonial avenue, the Mall. And then there was Paris, with the Arc De Triomphe at one end of the broad tree-lined Avenue de Champs Elysees, and the Palace of the Louvre, at the other.

The other question was that of architectural style. Neither Lutyens nor Baker had a good opinion of Indian architecture, and felt that it was European Classicism that could best represent the British Raj. On the other hand Lord Hardinge, who was the Viceroy of India at the time, as also George V himself, were more in favour of giving the buildings a distinctly Indian stamp. Hardinge, in particular, prevailed upon the architects at several points to put Indian features on the structures they designed.

New Delhi took much longer to execute than had originally been planned, mainly because the First World War intervened and necessitated a diversion of resources. The new capital was finally inaugurated on 10 February 1931. By then it was increasingly clear that the days of British rule over India were numbered. When India became independent on 15 August 1947, it was only logical and practical that New Delhi, though designed as a city for an imperial power, should be its capital.

THE WALK

All of New Delhi is of course impossible to cover in a single walk, but it is possible to take in the stretch known as the Central Vista. Though it is a long walk, it takes you through the major focal points of New Delhi.

India Gate (1) is the popular name for the War Memorial Arch, located off-centre in a large hexagonal space with roads radiating from it. The arch was designed by Lutyens and is similar to European memorial arches, notably the Arc de Triomphe in Paris. Finished in 1921, the arch commemorates Indian soldiers killed in the First World War and other wars such as the Afghan war. Look at the long lists of names inscribed on it. Within the side arches are set large stone urns with pine cones in them. These have symbolized death and regeneration in Western culture since ancient Roman times.

Below the arch is the Amar Jawan Jyoti, the 'flame of the eternal warrior'. Erected after the India-Pakistan war in 1971, it is a memorial to honour all Indian soldiers who lay down their lives to defend the nation.

'Here is the site where the palace of the Maharaja of Patiala is being built. There the palace of the Maharaja of Bikaner. Farther on the splendid residence of the Nizam of Hyderabad. The millionaires of Fifth Avenue are beaten by ten lengths.' (Maurice Dekobra, *Perfumed Tigers: Adventures in the Lands of the Maharajas,* 1931)

East of that is the chhatri or **canopy (2)**, which is placed in the centre of the hexagon. It was designed by Lutyens as a memorial to George V, who died in 1936. It held a statue of that monarch till 1968, when it was removed to Coronation Park in north Delhi. The primary inspiration for this concept are the baldachins that cover statues in European architecture, but it also has prototypes in India. The large shells set at the corners of the base symbolize Britain ruling over the oceans. There has been debate about what should be done with the canopy with suggestions ranging from placing a statue of Mahatma Gandhi under it to outright demolition! Fortunately it seems that it is here to stay, picturesquely visible from a distance framed by India Gate.

The original name for the area around India Gate is Princes' Park. The reference here is to the rulers of semi-independent principalities that existed in India during British rule. Some of the more important ones were given plots of land here to build 'houses', which are arranged along the road that runs around the hexagon. You might like to see some of these more closely, in which case you will have to cross the road at the pedestrian crossing at Rajpath, west of India Gate, and proceed in a clockwise direction. You will have to cross several radial roads as you make your way around; do so with care.

The radial road that is next to Rajpath is Ashoka road, and crossing it brings you to the grand and well-kept **Hyderabad House (3)**, designed by Lutyens and built in 1928. Recent alterations have detracted somewhat from its appearance. The now enclosed but originally open balconies and verandahs would have broken the façade up with deep shadows, making it more interesting.

The next radial road is Kasturba Gandhi Marg, and after you cross it, you come to **Baroda House (4)**. Designed by Lutyens and built in 1936, this building now houses Railway offices. Cross the next two roads—Copernicus Marg and Tilak Marg, and you will come to **Patiala House (5)**, built in 1938.

Then, after Purana Qila Road, you will find yourself in front of the **National Stadium (6)**. In Lutyens' original concep-

6

tion of the Central Vista, the view on the eastern side was to end in the Purana Qila, the sixteenth century fortress, reflected in a lake that would be created at the foot of its tall ramparts. In fact, what can be seen today is just the chhatris at the top of the fort's gates. This is because in the 1930s the National Stadium was built, much against Lutyens' wishes, between the fort and India Gate. This stadium was designed and built by the Public Works Department, which was actually responsible for many of the buildings in New Delhi including Connaught Place and most of the bungalows. Note the untypical chhatris on the roof—a quasi-Indian touch suggested by Lady Willingdon, the wife of the then Viceroy.

7

The radial road after this is Sher Shah Road and beyond it is **Jaipur House (7)**, which now holds the National Gallery of Modern Art. The domed building was designed by the English architect Arthur Bloomfield. It was built in 1936 in a popular 'butterfly-shape'. Note the very plain but impressive façade.

Another couple of roads (Dr Zakir Hussain Marg and Panadara Road) and you come to **Bikaner House (8)**. Another princely house, but built on a fairly modest scale, this now accommodates the Rajasthan state tourism offices.

Cross two further roads (Shahjahan Road and Akbar Road) and your circle is complete. You will find yourself on the wide strip of green that lines the central ceremonial road leading from India Gate westwards. This road is called Rajpath (the 'avenue of the state'), but its original name was Kingsway. Channels of water flow through the middle of the green strip along either side of the road.

In the green area to the left you can see a whitewashed building. This is an **eighteenth-century mosque (9)**. It should be remembered that the land on which New Delhi was built was part of the older 'cities' of Delhi or their suburbs, dotted with houses, places of worship and tombs. When the building of the new capital began, only the most important of these were left, the others were swept away. This particular area went by the name of Zabitaganj, named after Nawab Zabita Khan, a Rohilla chieftain.

Carry on beyond the crossroad, and the crossroad after that is Janpath, or 'the avenue of the people', originally called Queensway. On the north it leads to Connaught Place, the shopping complex built as part of New Delhi. Just south of its junction with Rajpath is the National Museum. Continue on your way along Rajpath, and you can see the big block of buildings straight ahead. As you approach you will also notice that the central, domed building is slowly sinking from view.

10

After the next crossroad, Rafi Marg, you approach **Vijay Chowk (10)** or 'victory square', originally called The Great Place. This was designed as an open space with large fountains, somewhat reminiscent of the Place de la Concorde on the Champs Elysees in Paris. Notice the stone railing that encloses it. It is on a pattern to be found at the ancient Buddhist site of Sanchi in Central India.

11

Ahead of you lie the twin blocks of the **Secretariat (11)**, popularly known as North Block and South Block. These buildings were designed by Baker, and constructed between 1914 and 1927. Baker had scant regard for Indian traditions of architecture, but said that he aspired to a 'style of architecture which would satisfy Indian sentiment, but would embody the high ideals of our rule in India.' What was left unstated here was the considerable pressure from the Viceroy Hardinge to incorporate Indian features.

So Indian features were in a sense tacked on, and the result is an interesting hybrid. Classical columns and domes

coexist with chhatris, jharokhas, jalis, carved stone elephant heads and pillars carved as if surrounded by bells hung on chains. The last was a feature of Hindu temples that was also borrowed by the Mughal emperor Akbar. As you walk up the ramp and into the space between the blocks, look at the central arch in the middle of each block. In proportions and features it is very similar, say, to the gateway to Humayun's tomb. One major difference is the shape of the arch itself, which is not pointed (as Indian arches invariably were) but circular. This was a point on which both Lutyens and Baker were adamant, despite the remonstrance of Hardinge.

Four slender pillars, the Columns of the Dominions of Empire, stand in the lawns in front of the two buildings. These were gifts from Canada, South Africa, New Zealand and Australia; territories of the empire with Dominion status. They are all alike, with a bronze sailing ship on top, signifying the maritime history of the empire. Immediately beneath the ship is a replica of the pillar capitals of Ashoka, the famous Buddhist emperor of India in the third century BC.

At the other end of the quadrangle stands **Rashtra-pati Bhawan (12)** or 'President's house', originally called Government House or the Viceroy's House, and built between 1914 and 1927. This large, handsome building is exactly the same size as Buckingham Palace, the residence of the British monarch, and has 340 rooms. Rashtrapati Bhawan and the Secretariat are located on top of a natural rise in the ground called Raisina Hill. In the original plan, only the Viceroy's house was to be placed on top of the hill, and thus it would be the most prominent building, visible

'The principle underlying the designs of the architects has been to weave into the fabric of the more elemental and universal forms of architecture the threads of such Indian traditional shapes and features as were compatible with the nature and use of the buildings.' (Herbert Baker, *India*, 1930)

from a long distance. Soon after, it was decided that the two Secretariat buildings would also be placed on the hill, at the same level as the Viceroy's house. It was a symbolic move, to elevate the whole machinery of empire, and not just the Viceroy.

It appears that this modification in plan was accepted by all concerned, but later Lutyens, who designed Viceroy's house, opposed it. This was when it became clear that when all the buildings were placed on the hill, this would cause Viceroy's house, which was set back from the secretariat, to sink from view as one approached the hill. By then it was too late to rework the plan and that was how it went through. The controversy however caused a serious rift in the relationship between Lutyens and Bakers, whose buildings, the Secretariat block were seen as having stolen the stage, so to speak, over Lutyen's great effort which was the Viceroy's house.

You normally cannot enter the grounds of Rashtrapati Bhawan, but you can see the building through its beautiful iron gates and fence. Notice the elephants on the stone posts that support the fencing. The large dome of the building has a flattened top and a projecting drum around its base, based on the Buddhist stupa at Sanchi. Much of the dome is covered in bronze which now has a dark patina of age. Below the drum on either side of the façade are two chhatris. They are placed close against the main building and don't stand out in the typical silhouette of Sultanate and Mughal buildings. Lutyens personally thought 'chhatris are stupid useless things', but as Hardinge insisted on them, he tried to design and place them so as to cause the least interference with the outline of the building. One interesting feature of the building are the fountains on the roof that are visible, at a little distance, on either side of the dome. The introduction of water as a functional and decorative element within a building was a very Mughal tradition.

In front of Rashtrapati Bhawan you will notice a tall, slender column, the **Jaipur Column (13)**. The land of the village of Raisina belonged to the Maharaja of Jaipur, from whom it was acquired. The maharaja made a gift of the column as a reminder of Jaipur's association with the site. The column was designed by Lutyens and is based closely on the pattern of famous pillars in Europe, for instance the Pillar of Trajan in Rome and the Obelisk in the Place de la Concorde in Paris. It did have some distinctive features though, such as the bronze lotus on top, crowned with a star. Lutyens designed this as a consciously Indian symbol.

'Whatever one's opinion may be of the aesthetic value of these palaces, one cannot help trying to discover the significance of this monumental display. One ends up by finding it in the necessity to impress upon the Indians, from the millionaire potentate to the starving sweeper, a respect for British power.' (Maurice Dekobra, *Perfumed Tigers: Adventures in the Lands of the Maharajas*, 1931)

14

If you turn back and walk towards Vijay chowk, on your left is a circular building, **Parliament House (14)**, originally Council House. In 1912–13 when New Delhi was being planned, it was thought that the very limited legislative council would sit in one of the rooms in the Viceroy's house. In 1919 however, Indian representation in the legislative council was expanded and it was realized that a bigger council house would be needed. Therefore this building was designed by Baker and built between 1919 and 1928.

Inside there are large chambers where the houses of Parliament meet, and of course many smaller chambers/offices. What you can see on the outside is a broad, pillared verandah. The dome is low and therefore all but invisible, particularly as it was decided to add another storey on top.

You are now back in Vijay Chowk. Before you leave, look at the large red sandstone fountains and the beautiful gardens that line the space.

GLOSSARY

Arcuate – in construction, that which uses arch-making principles.

Bagh – garden.

Bangla roof – a vaulted roof in the style of reed huts commonly found in Bengal.

Baoli – a well with steps leading down to the level of the water.

Bastion – a projecting part of a fort wall, aimed at providing an increased angle of fire.

Batter – a backwards slope in a wall, so that the wall tapers on top—a feature typical of Tughlaq architecture.

Battlements – top of a fort wall, containing arrow slits and/or merlons.

Cenotaph – gravestone at floor level, where the actual grave is at a considerable depth immediately below.

Charbagh – a garden divided into quarters in a grid pattern of walkways and water channels.

Chhajja – projecting eaves, usually supported on decoratively carved brackets.

Chhatri – domed kiosk, supported on pillars, usually placed on a roof.

Chowk – square.

Corbel – projection from a wall, supporting a structure above.

Cusped arch – also called a scalloped or engrailed arch, one in which the curved edge is indented with several small curves.

Dalan – an arcaded verandah.

Dargah – the tomb of a Muslim saint, or a shrine housing a sacred relic.

Folly – an ornamental building with no practical function, often mimicking an exotic or old building.

Gumbad – dome, or a domed building.

Gumti – small dome or a small domed building.

Hammam – bathhouse.

Incised plaster – limestone plaster carved and cut into decorative patterns.

Jali – screen, usually carved out of stone.

Jharokha – an oriel window, a decorative window projecting out of the wall.

Kalash – a Hindu ritual vessel.

Kalima – the Islamic creed which states that 'there is no God but Allah and Mohammad is his Prophet'.

Kangura – or merlon; an upright tablet-shaped construction, to be found in rows on top of a fort wall, behind each of which an archer or shooter can shelter.

Khanqah – a Sufi monastry.

Madrasa – an institution of learning, usually a college.

Merlon – see kangura.

Mihrab – literally arch; usually applied to the blind arches on that wall of a tomb or mosque that faces Mecca.

Minar – tower.

Minbar – pulpit in a mosque, from where the imam leads the prayer.

Mosalla – prayer carpet used by Muslims.

Naubat Khana – drum house located on top of a grand gateway, frequently attached to palaces. So named because of an open gallery on top that housed musicians who played ceremonial drums.

Qalamdan – literally 'pen holder', a ridge shaped piece of stone or masonry on graves of males.

Qibla wall – the wall of a tomb or mosque that faces Mecca, in India invariably the western wall.

Sarai – caravanserai, an inn.

Scalloped arch – see cusped arch.

Stucco – plaster coating often decorative; see also incised plaster.

Takhti — literally 'writing tablet', a flat ornament on a gravestone denoting a female's grave.

Trabeate – in construction, covering space using vertical columns and horizontal beam.

Wall mosque – a qibla wall with mihrabs, often next to a burial site.

Wazir – minister; in Mughal times usually the prime minister.

Wuzu – ritual ablutions performed by Muslims before prayer.

TIMELINE OF EVENTS

This is not meant to be comprehensive, but just a ready reckoner of dates of founding of cities, key events and reigns of monarchs that figure in this book, and during the period covered by these walk routes.

375–413 reign of Chandragupta II, during which the iron pillar at Mehrauli was set up.

circa 1060 Anagpal II of the Tomar dynasty founds the city of Dilli and builds Lal Kot.

1150s Chauhans displace the Tomars, extend Lal Kot to form Qila Rai Pithora.

1192 Mohammad Ghori's armies defeat the forces of Prithviraj Chauhan, and the Delhi Sultanate is founded.

1202 construction of Qutub Minar begins.

1206–11 reign of Qutubuddin Aibak.

1212–35 reign of Iltutmish.

1246 Balban becomes de facto ruler, with the king Nasiruddin Mahmud ruling as a puppet.

1265–87 Balban rules as sultan.

1290–1316 reign of Jalaluddin Firoz, founder of the Khalji dynasty.

1296–1316 reign of Alauddin Khalji.

circa 1297 Alauddin Khalji founds the city of Siri.

1320–25 reign of Ghiyasuddin Tughlaq, building of Tughlaqabad.

1325–51 reign of Mohammad Tughlaq.

1326–27 founding of Jahanpanah.

1351–88 reign of Firoz Shah Tughlaq.

circa 1354 building of Firozabad.

1398 invasion of Timur.

1414–51 the Syed dynasty rules a weakened and shrunken Sultanate.

1451–56 Lodi dynasty rules, leaving behind monumental remains in Delhi, but no new city.

1526–30 reign of Babur, who overthrows Ibrahim Lodi to found the Mughal dynasty.

1530–40 first reign of Humayun.

1533 construction of Dinpanah (Purana Qila) begins.

1540 Sher Shah Sur defeats Humayun and drives him into exile.

1555–56 second reign of Humayun, who defeats last Sur ruler to regain throne but dies within the year.

1556–1605 reign of Akbar.

late 1550s Mughal capital moved to Agra.

1563–71 building of Humayun's tomb.

1639–48 founding of Shahjahanabad and construction of the Red Fort.

1648 the capital moves back to Delhi.

1658–1707 reign of Aurangzeb who deposes Shahjahan to become emperor.

1719–48 reign of Mohammad Shah 'Rangila'.

1739 invasion of Nadir Shah.

1748–1803 decline of the Mughal dynasty.

1803 British East India Company occupies Delhi.

1857 Delhi is an important centre of the great uprising against British rule.

1911 the transfer of the capital from Calcutta to Delhi is announced.

1931 the inauguration of New Delhi as the capital.

BIBLIOGRAPHY

The list has been restricted to books in English that a non-specialist enthusiast may find interesting for further reading

Lucy Peck: *Delhi: A Thousand Years of Building;* Roli Books, 2005

Upinder Singh: *Ancient Delhi;* Oxford University Press, 2006

H.K. Kaul (ed.): *Historic Delhi: An Anthology;* Oxford University Press,1985

Carr Stephen: *The Archaeology and Monumental Remains of Delhi;* Aryan Books, 2002 (reprint of 1876 edition)

Zafar Hasan: *Monuments of Delhi;* Aryan Books, 2008 (reprint of 1916 edition)

Percival Spear: *Delhi: Its Monuments and History* (annotated and updated by Narayani Gupta and Laura Sykes); Oxford University Press, 1994 (originally published in 1943.)

M.M Kaye (ed.): *The Golden Calm: An English Lady's life in Moghul Delhi;* Webb & Bower, 1980

Percival Spear, Narayani Gupta and R.E. Frykenberg: *The Delhi Omnibus;* Oxford University Press, 2002

Stephen P. Blake: *Shahjahanabad: The Sovereign City in Mughal India 1639-1739;* Cambridge University Press, 1993

Shama Mitra Chenoy: *Shahjahanabad: A City of Delhi 1638-1857;* Munshiram Mano-harlal, 1998

Monuments of Delhi; Archaeological Survey of India, 2010

Mala Dayal (ed.): *Celebrating Delhi;* Penguin and Ravi Dayal, 2010

INDEX

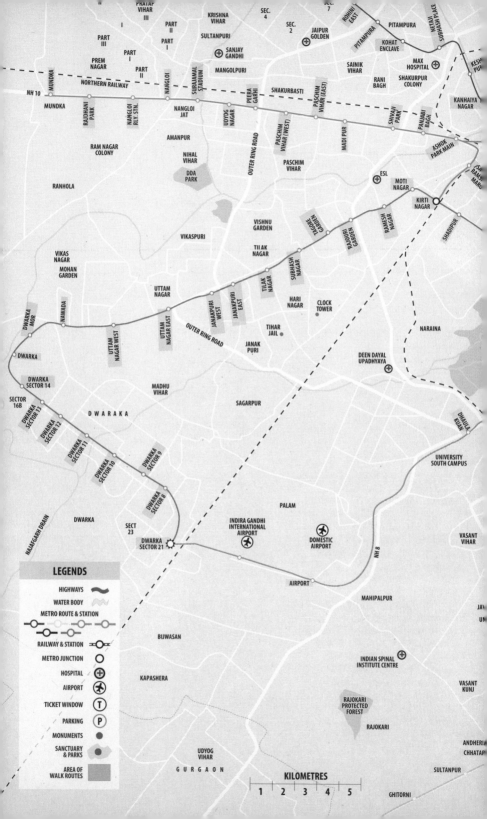

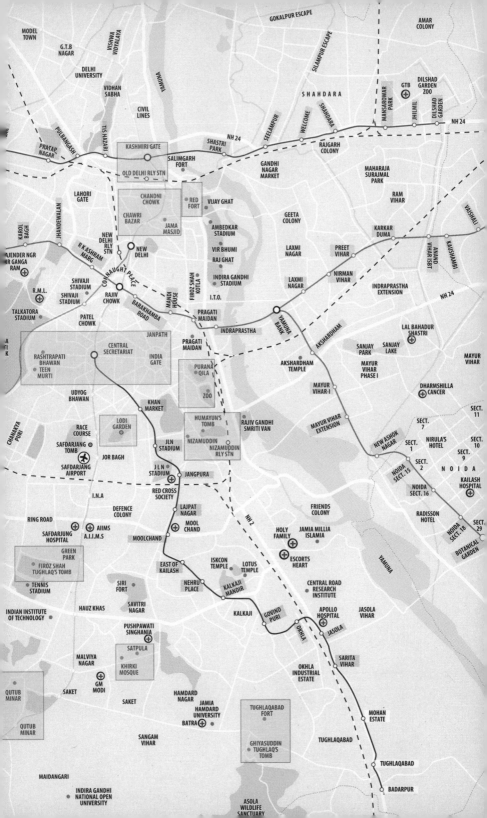